D1709539

Miranda v. Arizona and the Rights of the Accused

Debating Supreme Court Decisions

Carol Kelly-Gangi

Enslow Publishers, Inc.
40 Industrial Road
Box 398
Berkeley Heights, NJ 07922
USA
http://www.enslow.com

This book is dedicated with love to my husband, John, for his tireless support during the time it took to complete this book; to my parents, for their faith in me and their constant encouragement; and to my children, John Christopher and Emily Grace, for the inspiration they give me every day.

I would like to gratefully thank Ken Haas, Ph.D., my former professor from the University of Delaware, for graciously sharing his keen insights on many Miranda issues; a special thanks to my sister, Theresa Kelly, Esq., for all of her valuable assistance in tracking down important pieces of research for this book; and thanks, too, to Catherine N. Walto, Esq., for her thoughtful critique of the manuscript.

Library of Congress Cataloging-in-Publication Data
Kelly-Gangi, Carol.
  Miranda v. Arizona and the rights of the accused: debating Supreme Court decisions/Carol Kelly-Gangi.
    p. cm. — (Debating Supreme Court decisions)
  Includes bibliographical references and index.
  ISBN 0-7660-2477-6
  1. Miranda, Ernesto—Trials, litigation, etc.—Juvenile literature. 2. Trials (Rape)—Arizona—Juvenile literature. 3. Right to counsel—United States—Juvenile literature. 4. Self-incrimination—United States—Juvenile literature. 5. Confession (Law)—United States—Juvenile literature. 6. Police questioning—United States—Juvenile literature. I. Title. II. Series.
  KF224.M54K45 2006
  345.73'056—dc22
                                    2006011737
Printed in the United States of America

10 9 8 7 6 5 4 3 2 1

To Our Readers:
We have done our best to make sure that all Internet Addresses in this book were active and appropriate when we went to press. However, the author and publisher have no control over and assume no liability for the material available on those Internet sites or on other Web sites they may link to. Any comments or suggestions can be sent by e-mail to comments@enslow.com or to the address on the back cover.

Contents

Introduction

You have the right to remain silent. Anything you say can and will be used against you in a court of law. Anyone who has ever watched a police show on television can recite at least some of the now famous *Miranda* warnings. The warnings, which were aimed at informing a suspect of his or her rights, arose out of a 1966 Supreme Court case titled *Miranda v. Arizona.*[1] The case, narrowly decided by a 5–4 vote of the Court, and the resulting warnings ignited a firestorm of controversy that has been hotly debated for the past forty years—one that has involved members of the Court itself, Congress, civil liberties groups, the police, and ordinary citizens alike.

This book tells the story of how the case arose, how the Supreme Court ruled, and how the case has been interpreted, or misinterpreted, in the decades since it was decided.

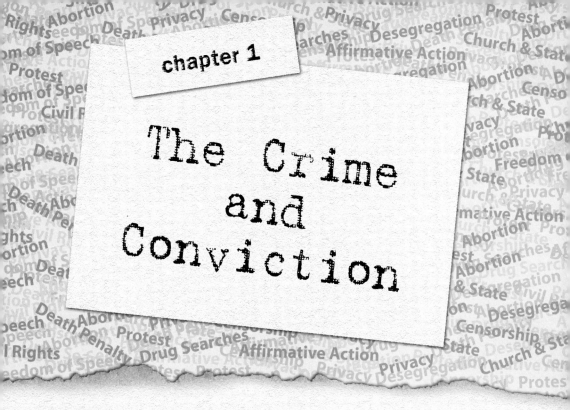

chapter 1

The Crime and Conviction

"Lois Ann Jameson" (not her real name) had no reason to believe when she left work on the night of March 2, 1963, that her life was about to be drastically changed. She finished up work at the concession stand at the Paramount Theater in downtown Phoenix, Arizona. As on any other Saturday night, Jameson took a bus with a coworker to go home.

It was after midnight when Lois got off the bus alone, and began walking the several blocks to her home. In an instant, a car pulled out of a driveway, almost hitting Lois. After traveling a short distance, the car stopped, and a man got out. He approached, grabbed Lois from behind, covered her mouth, and said, "Don't scream and I won't hurt you." He then dragged her back to his car, forced her into the back seat, and tied her hands and ankles. The man warned her to lie still as he pushed a cold, sharp object into her neck. After driving to the Arizona desert, the man raped Lois. He took four dollars from her—all the money she had—and drove her back to the area where he had first grabbed her. There he let her out, saying, "Whether you tell your mother what has happened is none of my business, but pray for me."[1]

Terrified, Lois ran the several blocks to her home and recounted the ordeal to her sister. She later called the police, who arrived quickly, and after hearing about the kidnapping and rape, they took Lois to a local hospital for examination. While there, she described her attacker and his car to the police. Specifically, she recalled a loop of rope that was attached to the back of the front seat of the car. This would prove to be a critical piece of information as the case developed.

Over the course of additional interviews, the police noticed inconsistencies in Lois's story. They asked her to take a polygraph test, which also proved to be inconclusive. The police began to doubt whether the rape had happened at all.

Within a matter of days, Lois returned to work at the theater. On March 9, 1963, while Lois's brother-in-law was waiting to walk her home from the bus stop, he noticed a parked car that seemed similar to the one Lois had described to the police. When Lois arrived, they went to take a closer look at the car. Although the car drove off before Lois's brother-in-law could take down the full license plate number, he had enough of it to contact the police. The police traced the number to a car owned by a woman named Twila Hoffman.

Later, the police went to Hoffman's address, but found no one at home. From the neighbors, they learned that Hoffman and her boyfriend, Ernesto Miranda, had moved a few days earlier. Miranda's physical description fit the one that Lois gave of her attacker. The officers ran a check on Miranda and found that he had been in and out of trouble with the law since he was fourteen years old. Through the post office, the police were able to track down the new residence of Hoffman and Miranda, and they went to the house on the morning of March 13. In the driveway, they noted an old car with a loop of rope hanging from the back of the front seat. The police knocked on the door. Hoffman answered and got Miranda, who'd been sleeping after working the night shift. The police asked him to go with them to the police station in connection with a case they were investigating, and Miranda agreed.

At the station, the police arranged for a lineup. They brought Lois in, but she couldn't say for certain that any of the men in the lineup was her attacker.

She did, however, feel that of the men present, Miranda most closely resembled her rapist.

After the lineup, police took Miranda into an interrogation room for questioning. Miranda asked one of the officers, "How'd I do?" to which one of the officers replied, "You flunked," despite the fact that Jameson had been unable to say for sure that Miranda was her attacker. The police began to question Miranda, who had no attorney present. The detectives later recalled that they simply questioned him and did not threaten or coerce him in any way. Not surprisingly, Miranda's recollection of the interrogation differed. He recalled,

> Once they get you in a little room and they start badgering you one way or the other, "you better tell us . . . or we're going to throw the book at you" . . . that is what was told to me. . . . They would try to give me all the time they could. They thought there was even the possibility that there was something wrong with me. They would try to help me, get me medical care if I needed it. . . . They mention first one crime, then another one, they are certain I am the person . . . knowing what a penitentiary is like, a person has to be frightened, scared.[2]

After two hours of police interrogation, Miranda confessed to the crime. He confessed to two other crimes as well: robbery and an attempted rape a month prior to his attack on Jameson. The police gave Miranda a form and told him to write out his confession. At the top of the form was a printed statement that one of the officers read to Miranda that said by signing the statement, Miranda was agreeing that his confession was voluntary and that he understood his legal rights. He signed his confession and was taken to the Phoenix city jail. At his arraignment two days later, he was formally charged by the judge with rape and robbery. Miranda later claimed that the police agreed to drop the rape charge if he confessed to the robbery. The police said they never agreed to do so.

It was at the arraignment that Miranda was assigned a lawyer to defend him at trial, since he could not afford to pay for a lawyer himself. Miranda was fortunate to have been assigned Alvin Moore, a seasoned seventy-three-year-old attorney who had been practicing for many years and who felt it was his civic duty to volunteer to defend indigent defendants, those who had no money to hire a lawyer to represent them at trial. Moore first decided to pursue an insanity defense for Miranda. However, psychological examinations revealed that although Miranda did have some mental problems, he did in fact know the difference between right and wrong, which was the legal standard for the insanity defense at that time. Today, the standard for determining legal insanity varies depending on the state.

At the trial, Moore focused his defense on the cross-examination of Jameson, by highlighting the inconsistencies in her statements and trying

Ernesto Miranda is shown in the lineup wearing the numeral "1." The police led Miranda to believe that the rape victim had identified him as her attacker, even though she had not.

to reduce her credibility, and on the cross-examination of Detective Cooley, one of the officers who had interrogated and elicited the confession from Miranda. Moore asked Cooley if it was his practice to advise people whom he arrested of their right to an attorney before they spoke with the police. Cooley answered that it was not his practice. Moore then asked the court to throw out the confession since Miranda had not been advised of his right to an attorney during the police interrogation. The judge denied Moore's request and in the jury instructions stated:

> The fact that a defendant was under arrest at the time he made a confession or that he was not at the time represented by counsel or that he was not told that any statement he might make could or would be used against him, in and of themselves, will not render such a confession involuntary.[3]

After five hours of deliberating, the jury came back with a verdict. Miranda was found guilty of robbery and rape. He was later sentenced to a term of twenty to thirty years at the Arizona State Prison.

Undaunted, Moore decided to appeal the case to the Arizona Supreme Court. In his brief to the high court of Arizona, Moore claimed that Miranda had not been given a fair trial, due in part to Miranda's illegally obtained confession. Moore reasoned that the police's failure to advise Miranda of his right to remain silent during their interrogation tainted the confession, rendering it involuntary, since Miranda would never have confessed if he had known of his rights.

In making this argument, Moore was relying in part upon a landmark Supreme Court case that had been decided in 1964, *Escobedo* v. *Illinois*. In that case, the Court ruled that defendants had the right to legal representation, if requested, immediately after being taken into custody. The Court further held that the police must advise suspects of their right to remain silent.[4]

In the end, the Arizona Supreme Court remained unconvinced by Moore's arguments. The court was able to distinguish the facts in Miranda's case from those of *Escobedo*. The court held that unlike the defendant in *Escobedo*, Miranda had never asked to see a lawyer. In regard to the failure of the police to warn Miranda of his right to remain silent, the court reasoned that Miranda was no newcomer to the criminal justice system; he was familiar with court proceedings and his rights under the system. In short, the court maintained that Miranda knew his rights and that he had freely confessed. The conviction was upheld.

Though Moore bowed out of the case at this point, Miranda decided to appeal the case to the United States Supreme Court, the highest court in the land. The case came to the attention of Robert Corcoran, the head of the Phoenix office of the American Civil Liberties Union (ACLU), which is a nonprofit organization dedicated to protecting constitutionally guaranteed civil rights and liberties. Through Corcoran's efforts, two well-known criminal lawyers, John J. Flynn and John P. Frank, ultimately agreed to represent Miranda in the case. In July 1965, they wrote to the Supreme Court asking the Court to hear Miranda's case. In November of that year, the Court answered. It would hear and decide Miranda's case—and settle the questions presented once and for all.

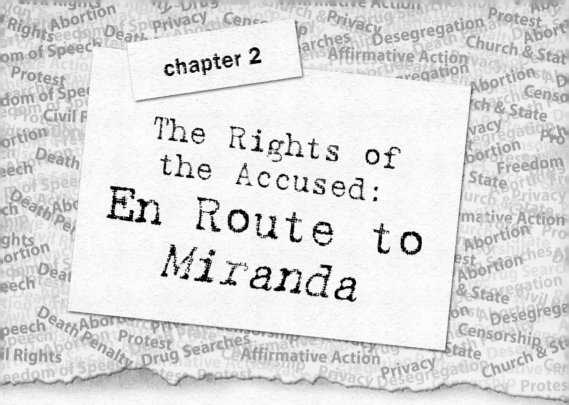

chapter 2

The Rights of the Accused: En Route to Miranda

During the medieval period in England and in other parts of Western Europe, the use of confessions played little part in determining the guilt or innocence of those accused of crimes. Rather, tests of physical strength and endurance were often relied upon, and procedures such as trial by ordeal were frequently used. This ancient legal custom required that the accused undergo a test in order to prove his or her guilt or innocence. The practice of ordeal was still used in parts of Asia and Africa up until recent times. The forms of ordeal changed according to the location and type of crime that had been committed. The types of ordeals included fire, whereby the accused had to walk through fire or put their hand into a flame (it was considered that if the accused was innocent, God would spare them); trial by water, which was often used to decide whether a woman was a witch and involved casting a bound woman into water that had been blessed (if she floated, she was considered guilty, and if she sank, she was considered innocent); and trial by battle, whereby one of the parties issued a challenge, and both agreed that the winner of the duel or battle would be awarded the decision. In 1215, the Roman Catholic Church forbade any of its clergy to take part in such activities.[1]

The importance of confessions grew, however, with the renewed study of Roman law in England and on the continent of Europe in the twelfth century. Since torture was commonly used in the Roman legal tradition, its use in connection with obtaining confessions became more widespread, especially in countries such as France and Spain, where there was a heavy reliance on the Roman legal tradition. In England, however, the development of common law (the system of law based on judicial decisions, customs, and traditions rather than on statutes and codes) reduced the influence of Roman law. As a result, torture was less widely used, though it still came into play for certain offenses until the Court of the Star Chamber was abolished.[2] Even after torture had long been made illegal, confessions were still extracted from suspects through physical force at times, but more often through the use of threats and promises of leniency.[3]

The Star Chamber

The Court of the Star Chamber was named after the stars painted on the ceiling of the palace of Westminster where the court met. It grew from the judicial proceedings typically carried on by the king and his council in medieval England and was separate from the common-law courts of the time. In the fifteenth century, its role was extended to cover criminal matters and it was later used as a political weapon to bring action against those who opposed the king. Its sentences included physical punishments, such as whipping, pillorying, and branding, but those convicted were never sentenced to death. The power of the court grew with each king's reign until finally its very name became a synonym for the abuse of power by the king and his cronies. It was abolished by Parliament in 1641.[4]

The right against self-incrimination arose during the reign of Charles I (1625–1649) in England, and the common-law rule against involuntary confessions came about later in the eighteenth century.

The first formal rule, established in 1783, stated as follows:

> A free and voluntary confession is deserving of the highest credit, because it is presumed to flow from the strongest sense of guilt, and therefore it is admitted as proof of the crime to which it refers; but a confession forced from the mind by the flattery of hope, or by the torture of fear, comes in so questionable a shape when it is to be considered as the evidence of guilt, that no credit ought to be given to it; and therefore it is rejected.[5]

Following in the footsteps of England, the early American settlers likewise prohibited torture and upheld the right against self-incrimination in the seventeenth century.

Protecting the Individual: The Bill of Rights

While the main body of the Constitution set up an ingenious system of checks and balances and laid out the framework for the government of the United States, it did not include much language that listed a citizen's individual rights.

On September 25, 1789, the First Congress of the United States proposed to the state legislatures twelve amendments to the Constitution in an attempt to detail the individual rights guaranteed to all American citizens. While the first two proposed amendments were not ratified (they dealt with the number of constituents for each Representative and the compensation of the

Congressmen), the remaining articles, as ratified by three-fourths of the state legislatures, became the first ten amendments of the Constitution, known as the Bill of Rights.[6] The Bill of Rights protected what the framers believed to be "unalienable rights" or "natural rights" of mankind. It included such rights as the freedom of religion; freedom of speech, press, petition, and assembly; the privilege against self-incrimination, and against being deprived of life, liberty, or property without due process of law; the right to an attorney and a trial by jury. It reserved for the states any rights or powers not expressly given to the federal government.

But did the Bill of Rights apply only to the federal government, or did it apply to the states as well? In 1833, the Supreme Court answered the question in the case of *Barron* v. *Baltimore*. The petitioner in that case argued that the state had taken his property without just compensation in violation of the Fifth Amendment to the Constitution. Writing for the Court, Chief Justice John Marshall held that the Fifth Amendment was not applicable to the states. In examining the framers' intent in drafting the Bill of Rights and the legislative history, he concluded that "these amendments contain no expression indicating an intention to apply them to the State governments. This court cannot so apply them."[7]

The Fourteenth Amendment

One of the post–Civil War amendments, the Fourteenth Amendment was passed by Congress in June 1866 and ratified on July 9, 1868. It was aimed at ensuring that former slaves would be granted automatic citizenship with all of the rights that included. The Amendment was also passed in response to the "Black Codes." These were laws passed by the southern states in an effort to bypass the guarantees of the Thirteenth Amendment, which had freed the slaves. The Codes were a new way for these states to control ex-slaves through violent means, and in essence, return them to their former station.[8] Section 1 of the Fourteenth Amendment includes important limits on the states. It says:

> All persons born or naturalized in the United States, and subject to the jurisdiction thereof, are citizens of the United States and of the State wherein they reside. No State shall make or enforce any law which shall abridge the privileges or immunities of citizens of the United States; nor shall any State deprive any person of life, liberty, or property, without due process of law; nor deny to any person within its jurisdiction the equal protection of the laws.

Beginning in the 1920s, the Supreme Court began to be concerned with the standards of basic and fundamental fairness with regard to criminal proceedings. First the Court dealt only with federal criminal cases; but later the Court extended this "fair trial" approach to state court proceedings in cases involving blatant and overt racism.

The first case, *Powell* v. *Alabama*, was also known as the Scottsboro Nine case. It involved nine young African-American men who were charged with the rape of two white women. The defendants were arraigned on the same day that they were indicted, and no lawyers were assigned to represent them until the morning of each trial. (Arraignment is the first step in a criminal prosecution, in which the defendant is called into court to hear the charges and enter a plea. In an indictment, the defendant is formally charged in a written accusation presented in court.)

With all the confusion, there was no time for the appointed attorneys to investigate the charges or prepare an adequate defense. The defendants were tried in three separate groups, and each of the trials was completed in one day. The juries found all the defendants guilty and sentenced them to death.

The Supreme Court carefully considered the circumstances of the case, including the youth and illiteracy of the defendants, the public hostility aimed at them, and the fact that they could be sentenced to death. The Court found that in this situation, the trial court's failure to provide the defendants with the time and opportunity to obtain counsel was a clear denial of due process.

(Due process is a concept rooted in the Fifth and Fourteenth Amendments to the Constitution. It means that the government may not deprive someone of life, liberty, or property unless certain legal rules are followed, including the right to a fair trial.) The Court went on to state that given the circumstances, the need for counsel was "so vital and imperative that the failure of the trial court to make an effective appointment of counsel was likewise a denial of due process within the meaning of the Fourteenth Amendment."[9] Though the Court was clear to say that this decision did not apply to all criminal prosecutions and all circumstances, it did hold that in a capital case (a case in which execution is a possible punishment), where a defendant is unable to secure counsel, it is the duty of the court to assign counsel as a "necessary requisite of due process of law."[10]

Several years later, in *Brown* v. *Mississippi*, the Supreme Court again examined whether state court convictions met with the due process requirements of the Fourteenth Amendment. In that case, three African-American suspects were charged with murder and were whipped, beaten, and tortured until they confessed to the crimes. They were then swiftly tried, found guilty, and sentenced to death. Witnesses openly admitted that the defendants had been whipped and beaten, and still the confessions stood. The Supreme Court, appalled by the facts of the case, reversed the convictions, exclaiming: "the rack and torture chamber may not be substituted for the witness stand."[11] The Court went on to state that

> it would be difficult to conceive of methods more revolting to the sense of justice than those taken to procure the confessions of these petitioners, and the use of the confessions thus obtained as the basis for conviction and sentence was a clear denial of due process.[12]

The Court had reviewed the record in *Brown* and found that there was no dispute that the confessions had been coerced and had not been given voluntarily. Thus, as a result of the decision in *Brown*, in future cases the Court focused on whether confessions were voluntary when deciding whether the defendants had been denied due process under the Fourteenth Amendment. While the facts in *Brown* included both physical and psychological coercion, in later cases, the Court would find that psychological coercion alone was enough to render a confession involuntary.

After *Brown*, when determining whether any given confession was voluntary, the courts would look at all of the circumstances or "the totality of circumstances" of a case and make the decision as to whether the confession had been given voluntarily on a case-by-case basis. Under this approach, the courts generally focused on three

Threats and promises of leniency were used to extract confessions from the accused, as during the witchcraft trials held in Salem, Massachusetts, in the eighteenth century.

factors: (1) the actions of the police; (2) the characteristics of the defendant (such as the defendant's age, education, and experience with the criminal justice system); and (3) the circumstances surrounding the confession. The courts examined and weighed each factor to determine whether the defendant had been coerced by the police into giving a confession. A court would be more likely to find a confession to be involuntary when all three factors pointed to the probability of psychological coercion.[13] (Of course, if the circumstances revealed the presence of physical torture, the confession would necessarily be deemed involuntary under the decision in *Brown*).

However, there are several downsides to the "voluntariness" or "totality of circumstances" approach. First, it can be seen as too vague for both the police and trial courts to follow. That is, it did not provide clear-cut guidelines for the police to know which tactics were permissible and which were not. They only knew what was considered improper in the unique set of circumstances presented in each case the Supreme Court decided. Similarly, the test did not provide clear guidelines for trial courts to use to assess the police conduct and the likelihood of coercion in any given case. Two trial courts could look at the exact same set of circumstances and come to opposite conclusions as to whether the defendant had been coerced and had confessed involuntarily.

Another problem with this approach is that the cases decided under the totality-of-circumstances test tend to have less value as precedents. (A precedent is a legal holding in a case that serves as a guide for deciding how future cases will be decided.) Because decisions under this approach are so closely tied to the facts of the individual case, it becomes difficult for future courts to apply the precedents to different circumstances. This becomes even more troublesome when a court is attempting to determine whether psychological coercion has taken place, since it is often a question of degree—that is, how far the police have gone to elicit a confession.[14]

Then in the early 1960s, the Supreme Court decided a series of cases that revolutionized criminal procedure and would become crucial links to the decision in *Miranda* v. *Arizona*. It was at this time that a process known as the Incorporation Doctrine came into more widespread use by the Supreme Court. This is a judge-made doctrine where certain provisions of the Bill of Rights have been held to apply to the states by interpreting that these rights were fundamental to the Fourteenth Amendment's Due Process Clause. The Court first used this doctrine in 1925 when it incorporated the First Amendment against the states. This means that the Court applied the provisions of the First Amendment to a state court proceeding. The doctrine was used more aggressively by the Court in the 1960s with the cases below, which incorporated important protections in the area of criminal procedure from the Bill of Rights against the states.

The first of these cases was *Mapp* v. *Ohio*. In that case, the police came to the home of Dollree Mapp looking for a friend of hers who was a suspect in a bombing case. She informed them that he was not there, and when they wanted to come in to look around, she demanded to see a search warrant. Later that day, they forced their way in by claiming to have a search warrant, and they found some print material that they deemed "lewd and lascivious." Mapp was charged and tried for possession of the lewd material. At her trial, the police were unable to show that they in fact had a search warrant when they searched Mapp's residence. Mapp was nevertheless convicted and sentenced to prison.

On appeal to the Supreme Court, however, Mapp's conviction was reversed. The Court held that because the police had searched Mapp's house without a valid warrant, none of the evidence retrieved could be used at her trial.[15] This rule, called the "exclusionary rule," had been in use in federal trials for years, but had never been extended to a state court proceeding. The Court based its ruling on both the Fourth and Fourteenth Amendments, stating that the exclusionary rule was "an essential part" of both amendments. In this way, the Court in effect incorporated the guarantes of the Fourth Amendment against unreasonable searches and seizures into the due process requirements of the Fourteenth Amendment.

Then, in 1963, the Court decided yet another landmark case where protections from the Bill of Rights were incorporated into the Fourteenth Amendment. This case would prove to be an even more valuable catalyst for *Miranda*. The case was *Gideon* v. *Wainwright*. In that case, Clarence Gideon was charged with breaking and entering a pool hall in Florida with the intent to commit a misdemeanor. Under Florida law, this offense was a felony (an offense punishable by one year or more of imprisonment). Gideon was indigent, and he requested that the court appoint an attorney to represent him. The court denied his request, stating that under Florida law, lawyers were appointed to represent indigent defendants only in capital cases. Gideon went on to represent himself at trial, doing the best he could given the fact that he had no legal training. Gideon was found guilty and sentenced to five years in prison.[16]

On appeal to the Supreme Court, Gideon's conviction was overturned. According to the Court's reasoning, the right to counsel is a fundamental right that is essential to a fair trial, and the failure to appoint counsel to defend Gideon was a violation of the Due Process Clause of the Fourteenth Amendment. In so holding, the Court overruled one of its earlier decisions in which it had held that counsel need only be appointed for indigent defendants in federal cases.[17] Relying on firmly rooted precedents and "reason and reflection," the Court reasoned:

> From the very beginning, our state and national constitutions and laws have laid great emphasis

on procedural and substantive safeguards designed to assure fair trials before impartial tribunals in which every defendant stands equal before the law. This noble ideal cannot be realized if the poor man charged with crime has to face his accusers without a lawyer to assist him.[18]

Gideon v. *Wainwright* marked the first case in which the Supreme Court applied the Sixth Amendment right to counsel to the states through the Fourteenth Amendment, and it would prove to be an instrumental underpinning to the Court's decision in *Miranda*.

The next key case building up to *Miranda* also dealt with the right to counsel, but in this case the Court went a step further than it had in *Gideon* v. *Wainwright*. The case was *Escobedo* v. *Illinois*. In that case, the defendant, Danny Escobedo, was taken into police custody for questioning in connection with the fatal shooting of his brother-in-law, which had occurred several hours earlier. The defendant made no statement at that time, and he was released after his lawyer filed the appropriate document in court.

Ten days later, the police arrested him again. On the way to the station house, the police told Escobedo that he should confess because a friend of his had already told the police that Escobedo had committed the murder. Escobedo asked to see his lawyer and did not make a statement. During the course of the interrogation, the defendant and his lawyer asked repeatedly to see one another, but the police would not allow them to confer. After the police brought in the friend who had fingered him, Escobedo finally implicated himself in the murder plot. At his trial, Escobedo denied his confession, stating that he had only confessed because the police had assured him that he would not be prosecuted if he just signed the confession form. The confession was nevertheless kept in evidence, and Escobedo was convicted and sentenced to life imprisonment.

On appeal to the Supreme Court, Escobedo's conviction was thrown out. The Court stated that the right to counsel would be hollow if it only applied after a suspect had already confessed to a crime without the benefit of counsel to advise him. The Court held the assistance of counsel is required under the Sixth Amendment as applied to the states through the Fourteenth Amendment when the following circumstances are present:

⟡ Police investigation turns from a "general inquiry into an unsolved crime" to a situation where the police are focused on a particular suspect;

⟡ the suspect is taken into custody by the police;

⟡ the suspect is subjected to interrogation, without being advised of his right to remain silent; and/or

◇ the suspect is not given the opportunity to meet with his lawyer.[19]

In so holding, the Court expanded upon the ruling in *Gideon*. Now, the right to counsel would not be limited to the trial but would also include the right to counsel during the interrogation phase.

The Court's decision in *Escobedo* was by no means unanimous. Several dissenting opinions were filed in which the dissenters attacked the majority opinion for indefiniteness and asserted that it would end up crippling the efforts of law enforcement. A dissenting opinion is an opinion by one or more judges who disagree with the majority's decision. Dissenting opinions are published along with the majority opinion, but they do not become law.

The decision in *Escobedo* ignited sharp public criticism. People were outraged, believing that the decision would handcuff the police and that the new requirements were vague.[20] In fact, the Court never actually said at what specific point in questioning that the right to counsel came into play. Questions remained: Were the police completely prohibited from private interrogation? What was the future of this longstanding police technique?[21] It would take the landmark case of *Miranda* v. *Arizona* to clarify some of the confusion that had been left in the wake of *Escobedo*.

chapter 3

The Supreme Court and the Miranda Case

The Supreme Court of the United States is the court of last resort in the federal system, meaning it is the highest court in the nation. Its members are nominated by the President and must be confirmed by the Senate. The Court is made up of one Chief Justice and eight associate justices who sit for life. The Court was established in 1789 by Article III, section 1 of the Constitution, which states that "the judicial Power of the United States, shall be vested in one supreme Court, and in such inferior Courts as the Congress may from time to time ordain and establish."

While the Constitution provided for several areas of jurisdiction for the Court (meaning the power that a court has to make a judicial decision in a case) its primary function was as keeper of the Constitution. The Supreme Court has two types of jurisdiction, known as original and appellate jurisdiction. The Court's original jurisdiction, which amounts for only a very small number of cases heard by the Court, generally involves lawsuits between two states, or between a state and the federal government. In these cases, the parties can bring their cases directly to the Supreme Court, which acts as a trial court in the matter. When the Supreme Court exercises appellate jurisdiction, it is usually reviewing the constitutionality of a lower court rule, decision, or procedure—one that raises what is known as a "substantial federal question." When the Court rules on a constitutional issue, its decision is just about final. Such decisions can be changed only by a constitutional amendment or by a subsequent ruling of the Court. When the Court interprets a statute, however, Congress can pass new legislation that is in line with the Court's decision.[1]

The justices have wide discretion in deciding which cases the Supreme Court will hear. More than seven thousand civil and criminal cases are filed with the Court each year. Of those cases, the Court reviews and hears oral arguments in about one hundred cases per term, while formal written opinions are given in about eighty to ninety of the cases. Another fifty to sixty cases are handled by the Court without the Court granting a full review.[2]

The term of the Supreme Court begins on the first Monday in October and runs through late June or early July. Each term alternates between "sittings," where the justices hear cases and give their opinions, and "recesses," where the Court writes its opinions. Generally, each side in a case is permitted about thirty minutes of oral argument before the Court. Up to twenty-four cases will be heard by the Court in any one sitting. Because the great majority of cases are appellate in nature, which means the Court is reviewing a decision from another court, there is no jury and no witnesses. For each case, the justices have copies of the prior proceedings and briefs from each side that contain the arguments of the parties. When the Supreme Court recesses at the end of June or early July, the justices continue to consider new petitions for review and prepare to hear the cases scheduled for argument the following fall.[3]

The Miranda Case

On November 22, 1965, the Supreme Court granted a writ of *certiorari* (ser-she-o-RAR-ee). This means they agreed to hear Miranda's case. The case was actually heard together with three others that presented similar legal issues. Each of the cases involved the admissibility of statements obtained

Legal Terms

amicus curiae—Latin for "friend of the court"; someone who files a brief in a case in which he or she is not a party, but has a strong interest. Such briefs let the court benefit from the added viewpoint.

appellant or petitioner—The person who feels the lower court made an error.

appellate court (also called court of appeals)—A court that reviews decisions of lower courts for fairness and accuracy. An appellate court can reverse a lower court's ruling.

appellee or respondent—The person who won the case in the lower court.

arraignment—The first step in a criminal prosecution, during which the defendant is called into court to hear the charges against him or her and to enter a plea.

brief—Written statement of a party's argument on one or more issues in the case.

concur—To agree with the majority in a court case.

dissent—To disagree with the majority in a court case.

indictment—The step in a criminal prosecution during which the defendant is formally charged with a crime by coming to court and being presented with a written accusation.

majority opinion—The ruling and reasoning supported by a majority of appellate court judges in a case. **Concurring opinions** are written by judges who agree with the majority opinion but have other reasons for their views. **Dissenting opinions** are written by judges who disagree with the ruling.

precedent—A legal holding that will determine how courts decide future cases.

writ of certiorari—An order granted by the U.S. Supreme Court when a party applies to the Court to review the decision of a lower court and the Supreme Court agrees to do so.

during private police interrogations in which the suspects were not advised of their constitutional rights or the police failed to obtain a valid waiver from a suspect of his rights, which meant that the suspect had not voluntarily, knowingly, and intelligently waived his rights. One of the cases was a federal case, and by ruling on the federal and state cases together, the Supreme Court would effectively wipe out the distinctions between interrogation practices at the state and federal levels.[4]

More than seven hundred pages of briefs were filed in Miranda's case. A brief is a written statement prepared by a lawyer that sets out the legal and factual arguments in a case as well as the authorities that support them. Many of the briefs in Miranda's case were filed as _amicus curiae_, which means "friend of the court." These are briefs filed by people who are not parties to the action but who have a strong interest in the subject matter. In Miranda's case, an _amicus_ brief was filed by the National Association of District Attorneys, which argued that suspects' rights had to be balanced with the public's right to be safe and that the Court should not hamper the police's ability to keep the streets safe. On the other side of the issue, the American Civil Liberties Union filed an _amicus_ brief and asserted that the Constitution and Bill of Rights protected the rights of all citizens, that the police should not be allowed to interfere with those rights, and that citizens needed to be informed of what their rights were. Finally, the attorneys general of close to thirty states filed *amicus* briefs arguing that the Supreme Court had no business getting involved in this matter at all. In short, they believed it was the domain of the states to enforce and oversee their respective law enforcement systems.[5]

On February 28, 1966, the parties made their oral arguments to the Supreme Court in the *Miranda* case. The attorney for Miranda, John Flynn, described the facts of the case for the members of the Court. He pointed out that the record indicated that at no time during the interrogation was Miranda advised of his right to remain silent or his right to counsel. In so arguing, Flynn was making the case that Miranda's Fifth Amendment right against self-incrimination as well as his Sixth Amendment right to counsel had been violated. At one point in the argument, Justice Potter Stewart asked Flynn what the police should do when the criminal justice system begins to focus on a particular suspect; what are the suspect's rights at that point; and who would know what those rights were. Flynn replied that a lawyer would be the only person to adequately advise the suspect of his rights at that point. Potter asked Flynn what those rights would be, to which Flynn responded

that he had the right not to incriminate himself;
that he had a right not to make any statement; that

he had the right to be free from further questioning by the police department; that he had the right, at an ultimate time, to be represented adequately by counsel in court; and that if he was too indigent, too poor to employ counsel, that the state would furnish him counsel.[6]

Stewart asked Flynn if there was any claim that Miranda's confession had been compelled or was involuntary. Flynn replied that it was the defense's position that Miranda had not been forced to confess "by coercion, by threats, by promises, or compulsion of any kind."[7] Justices Hugo Black and Byron White then got into a discussion about the circumstances under which a confession is compelled. Chief Justice Earl Warren then asked Flynn hypothetically if the police had gotten a confession out of the suspect by acting as if they were his friends and promising him they wouldn't prosecute if he confessed, would that amount to a violation of the suspect's Fifth Amendment rights? Flynn agreed that it would still fall within the protection of the Fifth Amendment. Justice Black asked Flynn if the Constitution protected *all* Americans. Flynn replied:

It certainly does protect the rich, the educated, and the strong—those rich enough to hire counsel, those who are educated enough to know what their rights are, and those who are strong enough to withstand police interrogation and assert those rights.[8]

Gary Nelson, an assistant attorney general for Arizona, argued for the state of Arizona. Justice

Abe Fortas asked him about Miranda's right to remain silent and to consult with a lawyer. Nelson urged the justices to avoid the "extreme" position of allowing suspects the right to counsel during the interrogation phase. Nelson explained.

> I think if the extreme position is adopted that says [a suspect] has to either have counsel at this stage, or intelligently waive counsel, that a serious problem in the enforcement of our criminal law will occur. . . .[9]

The Court also heard from Duane Nedrud, who was there representing the National District Attorneys Association as *amicus curiae*. Nedrud warned that if the Court was attempting to strive for equality between the police and criminals, it would be "dangerous ground." He asserted that if it was the Court's objective to limit the use of confessions in criminal cases, "then you are taking from the police the most important piece of evidence in every case that they bring before a court of justice."[10] Chief Justice Warren then asked Nedrud about what should happen when a suspect asked to see a lawyer before speaking to the police. Nedrud replied that if the suspect asks for a lawyer and does not waive his right to counsel, one should be provided for him, but that he should not be "encouraged" to have a lawyer. Warren pressed him, asking if he believed lawyers were a menace to our administration of justice. Nedrud replied that while a lawyer is not a menace at the level of the trial court, he is a menace if he prevents a confession from being obtained during interrogation. In response to questioning from Justice William O. Douglas about important rights being lost many weeks before a trial occurs, Nedrud countered:

> If the defense counsel comes in at the arrest stage, he will, as he should, prevent the defendant from confessing to his crime, and you will have fewer convictions. If this is what is wanted, this is what will occur.[11]

The Supreme Court decided Miranda's case on June 13, 1966. There were deep divisions between the justices about the case. Chief Justice Earl Warren spoke for the bare majority of five, holding that the prosecution could not use statements that a suspect made while being held in custody by the police and interrogated unless it could show that the police used procedures that protected the suspect's right against self-incrimination. The Court explained that by "custodial interrogation" it was referring to any time the police questioned someone who had been taken into custody or otherwise deprived of freedom in any serious way.[12] Thus, the Court showed that it was viewing the case as being about the right to remain silent or the right against self-incrimination (which is a right based in the Fifth Amendment) rather than being about the right to counsel (which is a right based in the

Sixth Amendment). The Court summarized the procedural safeguards as follows:

> We hold that, when an individual is taken into custody or otherwise deprived of his freedom by the authorities in any significant way and is subjected to questioning, the privilege against self-incrimination is jeopardized. Procedural safeguards must be employed to protect the privilege, and unless other fully effective means are adopted to notify the person of his right of silence and to assure that the exercise of the right will be scrupulously honored, the following measures are required. He must be warned prior to any questioning that he has the right to remain silent, that anything he says can be used against him in a court of law, that he has the right to the presence of an attorney, and that, if he cannot afford an attorney one will be appointed for him prior to any questioning if he so desires. Opportunity to exercise these rights must be afforded to him throughout the interrogation. After such warnings have been given, and such opportunity afforded him, the individual may knowingly and intelligently waive these rights and agree to answer questions or make a statement. But unless and until such warnings and waiver are demonstrated by the prosecution at trial, no evidence obtained as a result of interrogation can be used against him.[13]

In order to lay the foundation for why such intricate safeguards were necessary, the Court focused on the inherently coercive atmosphere that is present during custodial interrogation. In the majority opinion, Chief Justice Earl Warren referred to "third degree" tactics that had been commonplace in the 1930s in which suspects were routinely beaten and tortured in order to compel their confessions. Warren maintained that in order to eradicate such practices completely, clear-cut procedural safeguards were required.

The opinion went on to discuss the psychological coercion that was pervasive in custodial interrogations. It included passages from police manuals detailing practices used to undermine a suspect's right to remain silent.

Chief Justice Earl Warren led the Supreme Court from 1953 to 1969. During that time, the Court expanded protections for the rights of individuals.

Such practices included what we know today as the "good cop/bad cop" routine, in which one officer acts sympathetic to the suspect and the other one acts convinced of the suspect's guilt. Other methods were described, including tricking a suspect into confessing by using phony lineups where the suspect is identified as the criminal; downplaying the seriousness of the offense; discouraging the suspect from getting an attorney to save his family the expense involved; and interrogating the suspect for long periods of time in order to keep the pressure on.[14]

Moreover, the Court held that even without the third degree or the use of the police tactics that it outlined in the opinion, "the very fact of custodial interrogation exacts a heavy toll on individual liberty, and trades on the weakness of individuals."[15] The majority admitted that the facts of each case it was ruling on did not necessarily point to the confessions as being involuntary in the traditional sense. Nevertheless, in each case the defendant was "thrust into an unfamiliar atmosphere and run through menacing police interrogation procedures" in such a way as to make compulsion inevitable.[16] The majority went further to state: "Unless adequate protective devices are employed to dispel the compulsion inherent in custodial surroundings, no statement obtained from the defendant can truly be the product of his free choice."[17] In so holding, the Court adopted what is known as a bright-line rule. (This is a legal concept that refers to a judicial rule that tends to resolve ambiguous issues in a simple and straightforward manner, though sometimes sacrificing fairness for certainty). In the context of *Miranda*, the bright-line rule meant that a confession obtained by the police in the course of a custodial interrogation without the specific warnings was by definition compelled self-incrimination and automatically inadmissible.[18]

By its holding in *Miranda*, the Court made it clear that the protections of the Fifth Amendment do not vanish outside of the courtroom door. Rather, the majority stated:

> Today, then, there can be no doubt that the Fifth Amendment privilege is available outside of criminal court proceedings, and serves to protect persons in all settings in which their freedom of action is curtailed in any significant way from being compelled to incriminate themselves.[19]

While the Court plainly stated that it was deciding a constitutional issue in *Miranda*, it added that it in no way meant to devise a "constitutional straitjacket" with its ruling in *Miranda*. That is, *Miranda* left the door open for Congress and the states to come up with strategies or safeguards of its own that were "at least as effective" in safeguarding a suspect's Fifth Amendment rights. Unless this happened, however, the safeguards outlined in *Miranda* would be required.

The Court then applied its holding to the facts presented in each of the four cases. It found in each case that "statements were obtained from the defendant under circumstances that did not meet constitutional standards for protection of the privilege."[20] As such, the confessions in each instance were thrown out. Three of the convictions were reversed, and the fourth conviction, which had been reversed on appeal to the California Supreme

Court, was affirmed (that is, the defendant was found guilty).

The majority decision in *Miranda* was decided by the slimmest possible majority. Four justices dissented in *Miranda*, and three of them filed dissenting opinions. In the case of *Miranda*, these opinions articulated many of the arguments that set the stage for the decades-long debate that has gone on since the case was decided.

In his dissent, Justice Tom C. Clark asserted that the majority had gone "too far too fast" in its approach. He advocated following a totality-of-circumstances approach where the failure of the police to give a suspect the *Miranda* warnings would be one factor for courts to consider when determining whether due process had been violated, thus rendering the confession involuntary.[21]

Justice John M. Harlan was even more out-raged in his dissent. He argued that there was no basis to expand the Fifth Amendment's privilege against self-incrimination into the police station. Further, he asserted that there was no Fifth Amendment precedent for the Court's ruling. Rather, Harlan asserted that the due process standard, with its flexible and sensitive approach, provided adequate protection for judging confessions. From a policy standpoint, Harlan thought that the police would be unduly hampered by the restrictions in *Miranda* and that society would suffer as a result. He stated:

> We do know that some crimes cannot be solved without confessions, that ample expert testimony attests to their importance in crime control, and that the Court is taking a real risk with society's welfare in imposing its new regime on the country. The social costs of crime are too great to call the new rules anything but a hazardous experimentation.[22]

Finally, Justice Byron R. White argued in his dissent that the majority opinion lacked common sense. White saw no logic that under the majority opinion a suspect could blurt out a confession while in custody at the police station and have the statements deemed voluntary, while if the police were to ask him one single question, any answer would be seen as compelled because of the inherently coercive nature of station house interrogation, even if the suspect had been warned of his right to remain silent. White countered that it is possible to say the answer was involuntary because it was in response to a question, but that it defied logic to say the answer was compelled. White also asserted that the decision in *Miranda* left open important questions such as the meaning of "in custody"; whether a suspect's statements were spontaneous or the result of interrogation; whether the suspect actually waived his rights under *Miranda*; and whether specific evidence would be barred as "fruit" of statements that came from prohibited interrogation.[23]

In light of these considerations, Justice White said he favored a more flexible approach to limit police interrogations rather than the majority opinion's constitutional straitjacket, which White believed was rooted in a "deep-seated distrust of all confessions."[24] White added a chilling prophecy of what he believed would come of the *Miranda* decision when he stated:

> In some unknown number of cases, the Court's rule will return a killer, a rapist or other criminal to the streets and to the environment which produced him, to repeat his crime whenever it pleases him. As a consequence, there will not be a gain, but a loss, in human dignity. The real concern is not the unfortunate consequences of this new decision on the criminal law as an abstract, disembodied series of authoritative proscriptions, but the impact on those who rely on the public authority for protection, and who, without it, can only engage in violent self-help with guns, knives and the help of their neighbors similarly inclined. There is, of course, a saving factor: the next victims are uncertain, unnamed and unrepresented in this case.[25]

It is noteworthy that as opposed to the majority of prior confession cases, the Court paid little attention to the factual circumstances of each case in *Miranda*. Otis H. Stephens, Jr., a specialist in constitutional law, noted that in the *Miranda* case, the fact that Lois Ann Jameson was brutally kidnapped and raped "is totally overshadowed by the Court's preoccupation with the establishment of inflexible constitutional prerequisites, applicable at least in theory to police interrogation throughout the country."[26]

The reaction to the *Miranda* decision was fast and furious from all sides. While championed as a victory by civil rights activists, the decision was bitterly contested by police, prosecutors, and all those who believed in a "tough on crime" approach to law enforcement. Those opposed to the decision feared that the police would be seriously "handcuffed" in their ability to fight crime. Since it was believed that more than three-fourths of convictions for major crimes were linked to confessions, the prediction was that the decision would strike a deadly blow on the war on crime. According to Patrick V. Murphy, who was then New York City Police Commissioner, "If suspects are told of their rights they will not confess."[27] With the decision in *Miranda* and the scathing dissents that accompanied it, the stage was set for the decades-long debate of one of the most controversial cases in Supreme Court history.

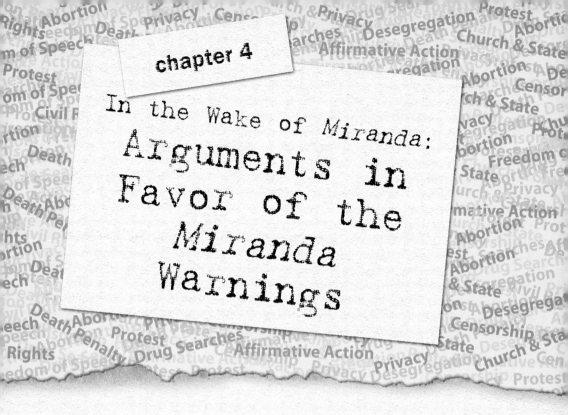

chapter 4

In the Wake of Miranda: Arguments in Favor of the Miranda Warnings

Proponents of the *Miranda* warnings assert that the warnings play a vital role in our criminal justice system. What are their arguments?

The Value of Confessions in a Criminal Case

It is clear that confessions are among the strongest items of evidence that can be introduced in a courtroom. Confessions have a very strong impact on jurors as well. Studies have shown that

> a confession has a compelling influence on jurors and they are more likely to convict on the basis of a confession than anything else, including eyewitness identification. This effect persists even when the jury is fully aware that a confession was coerced and likely nonvoluntary.[1]

The *Miranda* Warnings

The following is a comprehensive form of the *Miranda* warnings. Police officers typically carry a card that has the specific wording of the warnings as used in their state to advise suspects of their *Miranda* rights prior to their arrest.

1. You have the right to remain silent and refuse to answer questions. Do you understand?

2. Anything you do say may be used against you in a court of law. Do you understand?

3. You have the right to consult an attorney before speaking to the police and to have an attorney present during questioning now or in the future. Do you understand?

4. If you cannot afford an attorney, one will be appointed for you before any questioning if you wish. Do you understand?

5. If you decide to answer questions now without an attorney present you will still have the right to stop answering at any time until you talk to an attorney. Do you understand?

6. Knowing and understanding your rights as I have explained them to you, are you willing to answer my questions without an attorney present?[2]

Even in the case where a defendant who has made a confession to the police later retracts or denies the confession, alleging it was made under duress, it still may affect a juror's decision about the defendant's guilt or innocence. That is, jury members may be unable to fully understand why an innocent person would confess to a crime that he did not commit. This is especially true because many would-be jurors have no firsthand knowledge about what actually goes on behind interrogation room doors. Expert testimony may be required to educate jurors as to the circumstances that would persuade a suspect to confess to a crime he did not actually commit, but courts do not always allow such testimony at a trial.[3]

Given the extreme import of confessions in the outcome of criminal trials, supporters of *Miranda* believe that the protections afforded by the warnings are essential to help insure that confessions arising out of police interrogations are not coerced or false.

The Interrogation Process Today

In *Miranda*, the Court devoted much of its opinion to exposing police practices that were commonly used to trick suspects into confessing. At the time, the majority was relying on police manuals that dated back to the early 1960s. What about police practices today? Numerous studies conducted in the 1980s and 1990s lend more recent support to the claims of police behavior that the Court detailed in *Miranda*. These studies reveal:

> Police freely admit deceiving suspects and lying to induce confessions. Police have fabricated evidence, made false claims about witnesses to the crime, and falsely told suspects whatever they thought would succeed in obtaining a confession. They have lied about the suspect's culpability, assuring him that his behavior was understandable and not really blameworthy, or telling him that if he described what happened, the victim could be helped. They have falsely told suspects that they had physical evidence such as footprints, fingerprints, or semen, that a codefendant had confessed, that the weapon used in the crime was found, that the suspect failed a lie detector, and that there was medical proof of sexual molestation.[4]

Although deception is seen by some as a necessary evil in order for the police to get convictions of those guilty of crimes, researchers have concluded that police deception can result in innocent people being convicted.[5] James McCloskey is director of Centurion Ministries, a group that works to free people they believe have been wrongfully convicted. McCloskey lists the following forms of deception as major factors in cases of wrongful convictions: police lies on the witness stand, police pressure to coerce false witnesses, suppression of evidence helpful to the suspect, sloppy police work after the police have concluded a suspect is guilty, and falsified forensic science reports.[6] As the following shows, the combination of police deception and psychologically coercive methods of interrogation can have a disastrous result for suspects.

The Effects of Police Interrogation

Studies have shown that being interrogated by the police is a very stressful event. The isolation and confinement of the interrogation room have been known to cause a variety of reactions that may include "loss of contact with reality" and "a trance-like state of heightened suggestibility," which can result in the difference between what is true and false becoming "hopelessly confused in the suspect's mind."[7] Other studies have documented that fear, anxiety, trembling, shivering, sweating, hyperventilation, frequent urination, and verbal incoherence are also observed in suspects under-going police interrogation.[8] Sophisticated studies about the behaviors of suspects undergoing inter-rogation reveals that it is not just the mentally deficient who succumb to the coercive environ-ment of police interrogation, but rather "people of normal intelligence can and do falsely confess to serious crimes."[9]

What is it about the stressful experience of police interrogation that would make an innocent person confess to a crime he did not commit? Studies that have explored obedience suggest that ordinary people are likely to crack under pressure and conform when they are confronted with an authority figure in a coercive atmosphere. In a series of landmark experiments on obedience performed in 1961 and 1962 at Yale University, Dr. Stanley Milgram explored how average people would react when placed in a coercive atmosphere and confronted with an authority figure who commanded them to act in a certain way. In the experiment, ordinary residents of New Haven were told by a scientist to administer electric shocks to a victim who was in an adjoining room. The experiment revealed:

> Sixty-five percent of [Milgram's] subjects . . . were willing to give apparently harmful electric shocks—up to 450 volts—to a pitifully protesting victim, simply because a scientific authority commanded them to, and in spite of the fact that the victim did not do anything to deserve such punishment. The victim was, in reality, a good actor who did not actually receive shocks, and this fact was revealed to the subjects at the end of the experiment. But, during the experiment itself, the experience was a powerfully real and gripping one for most participants.[10]

How do such findings relate to the context of coerced confessions? In their writings on coerced and nonvoluntary confessions, researchers Hollida Wakefield and Ralph Underwager have concluded, "The result of such sophisticated and psychologically persuasive interrogation techniques is that many people will confess to crimes, even when it is against their best interests."[11]

It is important to note that there are two potential negative outcomes that can result from the coercive atmosphere present in police inter-rogations. First, a suspect may cave in to the intense pressures of the interrogation room and give a false confession (that is, a confession to a crime he did not commit), which could mean the conviction of a completely innocent person. Second, the suspect could give into the pressures of the interrogation room and confess to a crime that he actually *did* commit but perhaps without a full understanding of or an assertion of the rights that are constitutionally guaranteed to him under *Miranda*.

Given the sophistication of today's police inter-rogation practices, proponents of *Miranda* argue that suspects need the protection that *Miranda* offers now more than ever in order to balance the scales between protecting their rights and those of police officers, and the public interest in effective law enforcement.

Miranda Warnings Actually Assist the Police

Since *Miranda* was decided, many opponents have argued that the required warnings seriously hamper the police in their ability to root out crime.

Some experts, however, disagree and maintain that the warnings are actually an asset to the police. Steven Shapiro, legal director of the American Civil Liberties Union (ACLU), has said that _Miranda_ presents a "win-win situation." He states:

> It gives the police a clear set of rules to follow. If anything, it makes it easer to admit confessions at trial, as long as the police obey the rules. It is fair to defendants because it informs them of their rights. It protects the basic Fifth Amendment right against self-incrimination. And it promotes a sense of fairness, [and] integrity in the criminal justice system.[12]

Shapiro further points out that _Miranda_ has actually "simplified" and "rationalized" the system. That is, post-_Miranda_, courts do not have to scrutinize a multitude of factors in determining whether a confession is or is not voluntary. As a result, Shapiro maintains that many law enforcement professionals actually support _Miranda_ because it has "professionalized law enforcement" and has made it easier for them to have valid confessions admitted into evidence. In fact, Shapiro notes that when the Supreme Court was asked to rule on the constitutionality of _Miranda_ (in _Dickerson_ v. _United States_, discussed in chapter 7), the Justice Department filed a brief on behalf of the Federal Bureau of Investigation (FBI) and the entire federal law enforcement structure asking that _Miranda_ be upheld.[13]

Members of the law enforcement community also believe in the utility of *Miranda*. Joseph McNamara, former police chief in San Jose, agrees that overturning *Miranda* would be a disaster. He explains,

> Most police officers are wonderful people, but let's face it, they get their rewards for getting convictions, not for being scrupulous about obeying or protecting people's constitutional rights. And we can't depend on politicians and police chiefs because they're under pressure to project themselves as being so tough on crime. So it's really an essential role for the Supreme Court to say, "look, this is a democracy in a free society and we want good policing, but here's the limit to which the police can go."[14]

McNamara also revealed that the Fraternal Order of Police demand that when the police themselves are suspected of a crime they receive their *Miranda* warnings and the right to an attorney. McNamara asserts, "So why should people not get the same rights that the police themselves think are important?"[15] McNamara believes that overturning *Miranda*

> would send a message to the American police that might lead to all kinds of consequences on the part of some officers who already go too far, that they can do anything they want, and it's most important that the courts set the standards in a free society that, although we want to have justice and criminals convicted, we will not tolerate the kind

of police methods that used to go on before *Miranda* and that go on in totalitarian societies.[16]

Support for *Miranda* also comes from a former member of the law enforcement community who was directly involved with the case. Larry Debus is a former Phoenix police detective who was among the people who questioned Ernesto Miranda the day he confessed in March 1963. Debus believes that "the case changed the balance of power between police and suspects for the better." Debus further admits, "To be real honest with you, the cops had known all along that the things they were doing were wrong. It was just a matter of getting away with it."[17] Debus, now a well-known Phoenix defense lawyer, remembers that he and his fellow officers used tricks such as the good cop/bad cop routine as well as threatening to "throw the book" at him to get Miranda to confess. He states, "My recollection is that several of us had a run at him. We did anything we could to get him to confess and, after a while, he did. Persistence pays off, I guess."[18]

Miranda Warnings Have Not Had a Dramatic Adverse Effect on Law Enforcement

Perhaps the biggest argument that opponents to *Miranda* have alleged is that the police will be unduly hampered or handcuffed in their ability to fight crime because of the required *Miranda* warnings.

What is the evidence that supports this argument? Welsh S. White, Professor of Law at the University of Pittsburgh and noted *Miranda* expert, writes that data suggests that "contrary to the dissenters' expectations, the Court's decision to provide suspects with the *Miranda* protections has not substantially increase[d] the handicap on society."[19] To the contrary, studies indicate that *Miranda* has had "relatively little effect on law enforcement."[20]

One piece of research that has been relied on by *Miranda* opponents is known as the Pittsburgh study. In it, researchers looked at the detective division in Pittsburgh responsible for investigating serious crimes, including homicide, robbery, burglary, and forcible sex. The researchers found that while the police obtained confessions in 54.5 percent of all cases pre-*Miranda*, this figure dropped to 37.5 percent in cases after *Miranda*, showing an overall decline of 17 percentage points.[21]

While *Miranda* opponents have latched onto this figure, supporters claim the numbers do not tell the whole story. They say the conviction rate needs to be looked at as well. Are defendants getting convicted regardless of being given *Miranda* warnings? In fact, the researchers in the Pittsburgh study did look at the conviction rate for major crimes in the area at that time and found that it had remained steady. Welsh White has stated, "While the conviction rate is not the only indication of police efficiency, these figures certainly suggest that the decline of seventeen percentage points in the confession rate did not produce a dramatic impact on law enforcement."[22]

A more extensive study conducted at Georgetown University also supports the idea that *Miranda* has not had a major impact on law enforcement efforts. In that study, researchers looked at the rate at which defendants arrested for felonies and serious misdemeanors in Washington, D.C., asserted their rights before and after the *Miranda* decision. The study's overall findings were that not much had changed since *Miranda* had been decided. In fact, the rate of statements given to the police was "'remarkably uniform' at around forty percent in both the pre- and post-*Miranda* periods."[23]

Miranda's own case is likewise an example of how the *Miranda* warnings tend to have little negative effect on law enforcement's ability to get a conviction. After the Supreme Court decided the famous case, Miranda received a second trial. His confession to the police was not admitted into evidence. However, Twila Hoffman, his former girlfriend, testified that he had told her about the rape. Miranda was convicted and he received another twenty-year prison sentence. Miranda was paroled in 1973, but in 1976 he was stabbed to death in a Phoenix bar. Though his killer was not found, an accomplice was picked up that night. The suspect was read his *Miranda* rights in both English and Spanish.[24]

The *Miranda* Warnings Promote Fairness in our Criminal Justice System

Proponents of *Miranda* agree that the *Miranda* warnings are an important safeguard in promoting fairness and integrity in our criminal justice system. As Steven Shapiro of the ACLU has said, "Do we really want to live in a system and live in a society in which the law enforcement depends upon keeping people ignorant of their rights?"[25] Further, what would the message be to the police and society overall if the Supreme Court overruled *Miranda*? Addressing the symbolic value of *Miranda*, Welsh S. White asserts:

> Overruling Miranda would convey the message that restraints on police interrogation have been largely abandoned. Undoubtedly, this decision would change the relationship between the police and the criminal suspect."[26]

Supporters of *Miranda* fear that this change would likely be for the worse.

The *Miranda* Warnings Have a Constitutional Basis and Thus Cannot Be Overturned

A longstanding argument has been whether or not the *Miranda* warnings are constitutionally required. In their ruling, the justices of the Supreme Court said that they did not want to create a "constitutional straitjacket" with the *Miranda* ruling. After the *Miranda* decision, Congress passed a new statute stating that voluntary confessions would be admissible and that the warnings outlined in *Miranda* were not actually required, but were rather factors to be considered in determining whether a confession was in fact voluntary. However, it is of note that the statute did not make much of an actual impact. Steven Shapiro of the ACLU noted, "It has not been relied on by a single administration, Democrat or Republican, in the intervening thirty years."[27]

The Supreme Court ended the battle over whether *Miranda* was constitutionally required in *Dickerson* v. *United States*. The Court ruled that *Miranda* was in fact constitutionally required, and as such, could not be overruled by an Act of Congress. *Dickerson* will be analyzed in greater depth in chapter 7, but it is important to note that with the Supreme Court's ruling in *Dickerson*, opponents of *Miranda* can no longer effectively lobby for *Miranda's* overruling. Instead, they will have to hope that the Court continues to carve out exceptions to *Miranda* that further reduce its effectiveness.

chapter 5

In the Wake of Miranda: Arguments Against the Miranda Warnings

The opponents of *Miranda* have strongly voiced their opposition to the case since it was decided and continue to do so today. It is important to note that some critics of *Miranda* argue that the warnings provide suspects with too much protection and should be discarded in order to strike a more just balance between an effective criminal justice system and the safeguarding of the rights of the accused. On the other hand, other critics of *Miranda* think that the warnings provide suspects with too little protection and do not accomplish what the Supreme Court had in mind when the case was decided. Both sets of critics agree that *Miranda* has unintended, negative consequences that need to be addressed. The following is a review of what the opponents of *Miranda* have to say about the case and its effects.

Miranda Has an Adverse Effect on Law Enforcement

Despite the arguments of *Miranda*'s supporters, some scholars in the field take the complete opposite view about *Miranda*'s effect on law enforcement. These opponents point out that upon closer inspection of the data, a very different story is revealed about the impact of *Miranda*. As a former Associate Deputy Attorney General in the U.S. Department of Justice in the 1980s and a law professor at the University of Utah College of Law, and now federal district judge in Utah, Paul G. Cassell is perhaps the leading opponent of *Miranda*.

While Cassell acknowledges that it is quite rare for the suppression of confessions (that is, confessions that are ruled inadmissible at trial because of a *Miranda* violation) to lead to the release of dangerous criminals, other factors must be looked at to gain an accurate picture of the true effect of *Miranda* on law enforcement. Cassell points to the issue of "lost cases," those in which the police fail to obtain a confession because of the *Miranda* warnings.[1] In order to quantify the impact of lost cases or confessions, Cassell considered two different sources of data. The first is what is known as "before-and-after studies," which review the confession rates in various American cities before and after *Miranda* was decided. Each of the eleven cities examined, including Pittsburgh, Philadelphia, Washington, D.C., and New York County, reported a drop in the confession rate after *Miranda* was decided; most of the drops were in the double digits. (Cassell omitted the results from Los Angeles, saying that the results were unreliable since two different surveys were used.) Based on the results of the before-and-after studies, Cassell concluded that *Miranda* is responsible for a lost confession in approximately one out of every six criminal cases in the United States.[2]

Cassell also compared the confession rates in countries where the full range of *Miranda*-type warnings were not followed. By comparing the confession rates in these countries as compared with the United States, Cassell asserted that the impact of *Miranda* could be reasonably ascertained. He first looked at Britain, which gives its suspects an equivalent of the first two *Miranda* warnings only (i.e., suspects are told they have a right to remain silent and that anything they say can and will be used against them in court; but there is no right to counsel during interrogation and no waiver requirement). This comparison revealed that while the reported British confession rates (meaning that the police obtained incriminating statements from suspects) were in the range of 61 to 84.5 percent, the American post-*Miranda* rates were in the range of 30 to 50 percent. Cassell believes that it is reasonable to infer from these figures that a 16 percent drop in the confession rate took place in the United States after *Miranda* was decided. Significantly, Britain has since enacted warnings that are more in line with *Miranda* warnings (known as the Police and Criminal Evidence Act, or PACE) and the rate of confession has since dropped from over 60 percent to between 40 and 50 percent, which is similar to the post-*Miranda* rates of confession in the United States.[3]

In addition, Cassell compared the confession rates in Canada, where suspects were warned of their right to remain silent but were not afforded the additional *Miranda* protections. He likewise found that the confession rates were substantially higher than the rates reported in the United States, which, Cassell observed, could well be because the *Miranda* warnings are in fact reducing the rate of confessions in the United States.[4]

In his analysis of the existing data, Cassell estimates that *Miranda* has led to lost cases for close to four percent of all criminal suspects in the United States who are interrogated.[5] Calculating the actual numbers by using the above figure multiplied by arrest figures provided by FBI's Uniform Crime Reports (UCR), Cassell estimates that in 1993 alone *Miranda* was responsible for about 28,000 lost cases against suspects for violent crimes and 79,000 lost cases against suspects for property crimes.[6]

In addition to the above number of lost cases, Cassell also points to the high number of cases that will be plea bargained (that is, where a defendant pleads guilty to a lesser offense instead of proceeding to trial) due to *Miranda*. As Cassell points out, plea-bargaining is closely linked to the strength of the government's case. Since confessions have strong value as evidence, it can be argued that reducing the rate of confessions would increase a defendant's ability to successfully enter a plea bargain. Cassell estimates, again relying on FBI arrest figures, that in 1993 alone there were 24,000 pleas to reduced charges for violent crimes, and 67,000 pleas to reduced charges in property cases. In these additional cases, defendants received more lenient sentences due in part to the reduced rate of confessions.[7]

While proponents of *Miranda* may argue that the percentage of cases lost as a result of *Miranda*—four percent—is very low, when the actual numbers are presented as Cassell has done, it seems like a much bigger price for society and the victims of crime to pay.

It is important to note, however, that Cassell's findings put him in a minority position with regard to the majority of criminal justice scholars.

Stephen J. Schulhofer, Professor of Law at New York University School of Law and outspoken critic of Cassell's methods, states that Cassell's position "has not won overwhelming agreement from criminal justice scholars." He further states, "The great weight of the evidence suggests that the *Miranda* system, as currently administered, causes no *net* reduction in confession rates, clearance rates, or conviction rates."[8]

Miranda Is the Result of an Activist Supreme Court

It has been said that *Miranda* is a classic example of inappropriate judicial activism. Prior to *Miranda*, the rule that governed whether confessions were admissible was the same for nearly 180 years: Confessions were admissible if they were made voluntarily.[9] Gerald M. Caplan, Professor of Law at McGeorge School of Law and noted *Miranda* scholar, has said in effect that *Miranda* is nothing more than a product of its times. Caplan asserts:

> In retrospect, *Miranda* seems most understandable as an exaggerated response to the times rather than as an enunciation of a natural right mined at last from the Constitution. *Miranda* was a child of the racially troubled 1960s and our tragic legacy of slavery. . . . To many, the government itself seemed the cause of racism and poverty, and those apprehended by the police, armed robbers as well as civil rights protesters, were seen as victims rather than offenders.[10]

In *Miranda*, Caplan maintains that the Court went too far in an effort to balance the rights between the accused and the accuser. According to Caplan:

> The ultimate issue is whether the government proceeded fairly, in a proper manner, not whether the suspect knew his rights. When the interrogation is noncoercive and the answers voluntary, the Constitution should be satisfied.[11]

He further notes that the Fifth Amendment privilege against self-incrimination is "best understood as a denial to the government of the power to extract confessions forcibly and indecently, not as a denial of the value of confession."[12] Viewed in this light, the Court's finding of inherent coercion where police interrogation is concerned seems more a product of judicial activism than anything else.

Similarly, Kenneth Haas, Professor of Criminal Justice and Political Science at the University of Delaware, states: "*Miranda* strikes me as a classic case of 'feel good' judicial social engineering that makes people think that something is being done to deter police misconduct, but which actually does little to protect the innocent."[13] Haas explains further that when the Supreme Court decides a case, the issue is in effect removed from the political system, with the result that "the momentum for better ideas to solve problems through the democratic process is lost."[14] In this way, smarter solutions that may better promote the goals underlying *Miranda*, such as videotaping the confessions from station house interrogations, never gain widespread support, since it is believed that the problems in the area of police interrogation have already been effectively addressed by *Miranda*.[15]

Miranda Warnings Are Not Effective Because a Majority of Suspects Waive Their Miranda Rights

The effectiveness of the *Miranda* warnings has been challenged again and again because suspects are most likely to waive their rights and speak to the police anyway. The simple fact is, between 78 and 96 percent of suspects waive their *Miranda* rights and willingly submit to police interrogation.[16] In light of this, many critics agree that the protections offered and waived really amount to no protection at all. George C. Thomas, Professor of Law at Rutgers University, notes, "Nothing seems to quench the desire of many suspects to waive *Miranda* so they can 'tell their side of the story.'"[17] In fact, according to David Simon, a reporter for *The Baltimore Sun* who followed a shift of detectives for a year and chronicled their day-to-day activities in his book, *Homicide: A Year on the*

Killing Streets, the reality of modern police interrogation is one in which

> a confession is compelled, provoked, and manipulated from a suspect by a detective who has been trained in a genuinely deceitful art. That is the essence of interrogation, and those who believe that a straightforward conversation between a cop and a criminal—devoid of any treachery—is going to solve a crime are somewhere beyond naïve.[18]

The *Miranda* warnings, Thomas says, have become nothing more than "pieces of furniture in the interrogation room."[19] In fact, even when a suspect asks to see a lawyer, a good detective will be able to continue to maneuver the suspect to continue speaking. For example, if a suspect asks to see his lawyer, a detective could counter with, "Why would you need a lawyer if you don't have anything to do with this?" or "If you want a lawyer, then I'm not going to be able to do anything for you."[20]

Miranda Does Nothing to Protect Against False Confessions

Richard Leo, Associate Professor of Criminology and Psychology at the University of California, Irvine, takes the *Miranda* debate in another direction when he analyzes the impact of *Miranda* on false confessions. Leo points out, "However unlikely or implausible it may seem, false confessions to police are not uncommon;

instead, they appear to occur with troubling, if unquantifiable, frequency."[21]

The problem with *Miranda*, in Leo's view, is that it basically has no effect on the conditions of police interrogation that lead to false confessions from innocent suspects. Why is this the case? Leo suggests that *Miranda* is concerned only with the "procedural fairness of the interrogation process" rather with the "substantive truth of the interrogation outcome."[22] As stated, this is supported by the fact that anywhere from 78 to 96 percent of suspects waive their *Miranda* rights and agree to police questioning.[23] What is even more alarming is that the suspects most likely to invoke their rights to put an end to police questioning are suspects with prior criminal records who are savvy about the process and their rights. The suspects *least* likely to invoke their *Miranda* rights, some of whom will go on to give a false confession of guilt to police after enduring the rigors of interrogation, are people who do not have criminal records and are inexperienced with the criminal justice process.[24] Leo concludes:

> Once issued and waived, *Miranda* does not restrict deceptive or suggestive police tactics, manipulative interrogation strategies, hostile or overbearing questioning styles, lengthy confinement, or any of the inherently stressful conditions of modern accusatorial interrogation that may lead the innocent to confess.[25]

Leo further points out that because of *Miranda*, trial courts have shifted their emphasis away from attempting to determine whether a confession was voluntary, and instead now focus on whether the *Miranda* waiver was obtained voluntarily. Leo's own observations support the notion that a trial court will almost always find a confession to be voluntary if the *Miranda* procedures were correctly followed.[26] This means that *Miranda* eliminates whatever protection suspects may have gained from having the court carefully examine a confession to determine whether it appears to be truthful.

The resulting scenario is one in which seasoned criminals may end up being the beneficiaries of *Miranda*, while innocent suspects are left to face all of the sophisticated, deceptive, and manipulative police interrogation techniques with no protection whatsoever.

Miranda Has Reduced the Criminal Justice System to a "Sporting Theory" of Justice

The notion behind the so-called "Sporting Theory" of justice, also called "the fox-hunter's reason," is that the suspect in a criminal case must be given some chance for escape, like a fox during a fox hunt. Gerald M. Caplan explains that in the context of the criminal justice system, this theory says fairness requires that "the police and the criminal should be on roughly equal footing and the rules of the game should be drawn to avoid favoring one side or the other."[27]

What is the problem with this approach? According to Caplan, allowing a suspect to have counsel present during police questioning gives too much of an advantage to the suspect. Caplan notes, "If the police are too formidable for the average offender, a lawyer will be too formidable for the average investigator."[28] Not only does this approach reduce the criminal justice system to a game, but it is a game in which the government is at a distinct disadvantage.

Likewise, Judge Harold J. Rothwax, a judge in the New York State Court system for twenty-five years, agrees that *Miranda* is nothing more than an example of the sporting theory of justice. He inquires, "Why would we try to advocate equality between a defendant and a police officer—unless we thought the system was a game, a sport, a fox hunt?" He further notes, "The purpose of the police station is far different from the purpose of the courthouse. It should be obvious that interrogation and trial have disparate goals."[29] Rothwax explains that whereas in a court room, under an adversarial system, equality between the parties furthers the interest of accurate fact-finding, equality between the police and suspect in an interrogation room instead obstructs the goal of truth because by its very nature, police interrogation "involves one party trying to learn the truth from another party who is not inclined to reveal it."[30] Judge Rothwax thinks that some people believe that because some suspects are sophisticated enough to evade justice, all suspects should be likewise given that edge. Rothwax counters, "It should be a source of regret that some guilty suspects are resourceful enough to evade detection and conviction. What purpose is served in the equal acquittal of the guilty?"[31]

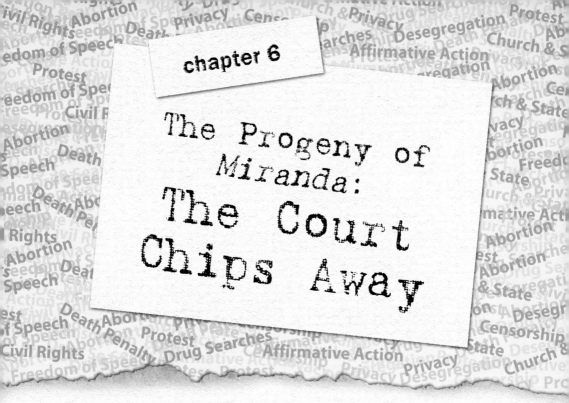

chapter 6

The Progeny of Miranda: The Court Chips Away

With the decision in *Miranda*, opponents were quick to levy criticism at the "activist" Warren Court for being soft on crime. In the 1968 presidential campaign, Richard Nixon made it clear that, if elected, he would strive to appoint new members to the Supreme Court who would be concerned less with the rights of criminal defendants and more with law and order. Nixon's first appointee, Warren Burger, came to the Court in 1969, replacing the retiring Chief Justice Earl Warren. In the coming years, additional Nixon appointees joined the bench. Harry A. Blackmun, Lewis F. Powell, and William H. Rehnquist, together with Burger, came to make up what became known as the Nixon Court.

What did this mean for *Miranda*? While the Court could not overtly overrule the case without coming into conflict with the rule of precedent, what it could do was chip away at its protections and, in effect, narrow its effectiveness. Beginning in the 1970s, the Court began to carve out exceptions to the *Miranda* ruling in a series of cases.

The first of these cases was *Harris v. New York* where the Court, in a 5–4 vote, held that while statements made in the course of a police interrogation before the defendant was given his *Miranda* rights could not be used as evidence against him, such statements could be used to impeach the defendant's credibility (call his truthfulness into question) if he took the stand in his own defense and made statements that were inconsistent with his previous confession.[1] The Court determined that the non-Mirandized statements could be used to impeach the defendant where the jury was told that such statements were to be used to judge the defendant's credibility only, and not as evidence of his guilt. This means that the prosecution could not use the evidence when presenting its case against the defendant. However, if the defendant decided to take the stand in his own defense, the prosecution could raise the matter in its cross-examination in order to point out that the defendant made conflicting statements and thus call into question his truthfulness.

In the 1974 case of *Michigan* v. *Tucker*, the police had arrested the defendant for rape and gave him some of the *Miranda* warnings, but failed to advise him that if he could not afford counsel, it would be provided for him free of charge. During the course of the interrogation, the defendant identified a witness to support his alibi for the time of the rape. When the police contacted the witness, however, he provided information that instead incriminated the defendant.

Despite the *Miranda* violation, the Court upheld the conviction. Rehnquist, writing for five members of the Court, reasoned that there was no bad faith on the part of the police—they had not acted in a willful or negligent way to deprive the defendant of his rights. The Court relied on the reasoning from *Harris*, that the failure to give the full *Miranda* warning does not bar the use of statements in every context. In now-famous language, Rehnquist declared that the *Miranda* warnings "were not themselves rights protected by the Constitution but were instead measures to insure that the right against compulsory self-incrimination was protected."[2] In *Tucker*, the Court also referred to the *Miranda* warnings as "procedural rules" or "prophylactic standards."[3] (A prophylactic rule is one made by a court to safeguard a right protected by the Constitution.) With this language, the Court further blurred the constitutional status of the *Miranda* warnings.

Form 2000-66-D
Rev. Nov. 59

CITY OF PHOENIX, ARIZONA
POLICE DEPARTMENT

Witness/Suspect
Statement

SUBJECT: RAPE   D.R. 63-08380

STATEMENT OF: ERNEST ARTHER MIRANDA

TAKEN BY: C Cooley #413 - W. Young #182

DATE: 3-13-63   TIME: 1 30/ Pm   PLACE TAKEN: Interr Rm #2

I, _____, do hereby swear that I make this statement voluntarily and of my own free will, with no threats, coercion, or promises of immunity, and with full knowledge of my legal rights, understanding any statement I make may be used against me.

I, _____, am 23 years of age and have completed the 8th grade in school.

Seen a Girl walking up street stopped a little ahead of her got out of car walked Towards her grabbed her by the arm and asked to get in

...

sorry for ... her to say a prayer for me.

I have read and understand the foregoing statement and hereby swear to its truthfulness.

WITNESS: _____
Wilfred M. Young #182

Ernesto Miranda's signed confession. Opponents of the Miranda warnings say that it reduces the likelihood that a suspect will confess, depriving the judicial system of a key tool in getting convictions.

The Supreme Court carved out another exception to *Miranda* in the 1975 case of *Oregon* v. *Hass*. In that case, the defendant was given his *Miranda* warnings and asserted his right to counsel. The police refused, however, to honor his request and continued the interrogation. Here, again, the Court ruled that the statements could be used for the purposes of impeachment.[4] The Court followed the reasoning set forth in *Harris* and held that the statements were allowable for impeachment, even though in this case the defendant had actually asserted his right to counsel as opposed to *Harris*, where the police had failed to give the full *Miranda* warnings. The Court was not troubled by this factual distinction.[5] The dissenting justices in *Hass* argued that the majority had gone too far to undermine *Miranda*. They said the police now had "almost no incentive" to uphold a defendant's request for counsel pursuant to *Miranda*.[6] That is, if the police continued to question a suspect after he has requested counsel, the worst-case scenario would be that they might obtain a confession that was inadmissible as evidence in the prosecutor's case but would be allowed during the cross-examination of the defendant if the defendant chose to take the stand in his own defense.

In 1984, the Court carved out yet another exception to *Miranda*. The case was *New York* v. *Quarles*, and the exception has come to be known as the public safety exception. In that case, a woman told two police officers that she had just been raped by an armed man who fled into a supermarket. One of the police officers caught the suspect in the store and asked him, "Where's the gun?" before reading the suspect his *Miranda* rights. The suspect pointed and told the police, "the gun is over there." The officer found the loaded gun, arrested Quarles, and read him his rights.[7] The Court held that the public safety concerns in locating the gun justified the police officers' failure to give the suspect his *Miranda* warnings before asking about the location of the weapon. The Court ruled that both the unwarned statement and the gun itself were admissible in the prosecution's case under a public safety exception. The majority reasoned that "so long as the gun was concealed somewhere in the supermarket, it posed more than one danger to the public safety; an accomplice might make use of it, or a customer or employee might later come upon it."[8]

Less than a year after *Quarles* was decided, the Supreme Court decided *Oregon* v. *Elstad*, which carved out still another exception to *Miranda*. In that case, the police went to the home of an eighteen-year-old, Michael Elstad, who was the suspect in the $150,000 burglary of a neighbor's home. The police met Elstad's mother and asked to speak to her son. In their living room, the police asked Elstad if he knew anything about the burglary

"Fruits of the Poisonous Tree"

According to this doctrine, evidence (the "fruit") derived from an illegal search, arrest, or interrogation is generally not admissible against the defendant because it has been tainted by the illegality ("the poisonous tree").

before reading him his *Miranda* rights. He admitted, "Yes, I was there." He was arrested and taken to the police station, where he was read his rights and confessed again. Elstad was convicted of the burglary, but his conviction was reversed on appeal. The appellate court reasoned that the second confession was tainted because the first confession was illegally obtained. The Supreme Court reversed the decision and upheld Elstad's conviction.

Writing for the majority, Justice Sandra Day O'Connor reasoned that exceptions that had been carved out from *Miranda* also applied to this instance, where the "fruit" of the unintended *Miranda* violation was the suspect's own testimony.[9] She wrote: "A suspect who has once responded to unwarned yet uncoercive questioning is not thereby disabled from waiving his rights and confessing after he has been given the requisite *Miranda* warnings."[10] The dissenting justices countered that the majority was engaging in a "studied campaign to strip the *Miranda* decision piecemeal and to undermine the rights *Miranda* sought to secure."[11]

According to *Miranda* expert Yale Kamisar, the *Elstad* majority seems to be saying that

> . . . a violation of *Miranda* is not a violation of a *real* constitutional right, but only a procedural safeguard or prophylactic rule designed to protect a constitutional right. Therefore, unlike evidence derived from an unreasonable search or a coerced confession (in the traditional due process sense)—which *are* real constitutional violations—it is not entitled to, or worthy of, the "fruit of the poisonous tree" doctrine.[12]

The watering down of *Miranda* considerably narrowed the protections outlined by Chief Justice Warren. This made supporters of *Miranda* more discouraged than ever in the late 1990s. It also gave opponents hope that *Miranda* would soon meet its demise. When in 1999 the Court decided to hear *Dickerson* v. *United States*, court-watchers saw it as the perfect opportunity for the Court to either finally overturn *Miranda* or to reconcile the growing list of exceptions that had been carved out of the case over the years.[13] But *Dickerson* created even more confusion than it resolved, and it has been sharply criticized by *Miranda* supporters and opponents alike.

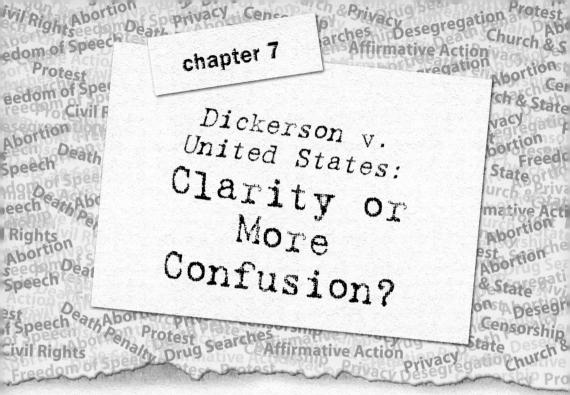

chapter 7

Dickerson v. United States: Clarity or More Confusion?

Two years after *Miranda* was decided, Congress struck back. Congress amended Title 18 of the United States Code by adding a new section, known as section 3501, entitled "Admissibility of Confessions." What this appeared to do was make the pre-*Miranda* voluntariness test the standard once again for the admissibility of confessions in federal prosecutions.[1] It stated that the *Miranda* warnings were not absolutely required, but were merely among a list of factors to consider in determining whether a confession was voluntary. In effect, section 3501 was an attempt to nullify or overrule *Miranda* through legislation. Not one law professor was invited to testify at the subcommittee hearings on the need or constitutionality of section 3501. But when Joseph Tydings, a leading senator in opposition to the bill at the time, asked more than two hundred law professors their opinions on section 3501, not a single one defended the constitutionality of the provision.[2]

At the time section 3501 was debated and enacted into law, it was called a "bald Congressional attempt to rap the Supreme Court's knuckles over crime."[3] But what was the long-term impact of section 3501? In 1976, Judge Henry Friendly in the U.S. Department of Justice Bicentennial Lecture series noted that section 3501 had

> not provoked the head-on collision that might have been predicted . . . The Attorney General . . . instructed his subordinates not to rely on it where it differed from *Miranda*, and although a later Attorney General changed this as official policy, most United States Attorneys appear in practice to have continued to take the restrained position initially directed.[4]

Indeed, as previously stated, Steven Shapiro, legal director of the American Civil Liberties Union, asserted in a televised debate in 2000 that after section 3501 was enacted in 1968, it was not relied on by any administration for thirty years.[5]

Dickerson v. United States

In *Dickerson* v. *United States*, the Supreme Court had to decide whether *Miranda* or section 3501 was the law of the land. In that case, Charles Dickerson was indicted for bank robbery, conspiracy to commit bank robbery, and using a firearm while committing a violent crime. This was all in violation of Title 18 of the U.S. Code, which included section 3501 regarding the "Admissibility of Confessions."

Before the trial, Dickerson made a motion to suppress a statement he had made to FBI agents on the basis that he had not received his *Miranda* warnings prior to the interrogation. The District Court granted the motion to suppress, but the government appealed the case to the United States Court of Appeals for the Fourth Circuit. The government did not argue the applicability of section 3501 (since the Justice Department, as stated, universally ignored this provision). Instead, two organizations representing crime victims and law enforcement filed an *amicus* brief arguing that the court should rule that section 3501 in effect overruled *Miranda*.[6] In *United States* v. *Dickerson*, the Fourth Circuit held that 18 U.S.C. section 3501 did overrule *Miranda*. The court reasoned that since *Miranda* was not a constitutional holding, Congress's enactment of section 3501 was the last say on the issue of admissibility in the case.[7]

The Supreme Court found itself in a sticky position. If it decided that *Miranda* was not constitutionally required, but was merely an exercise of the Court's supervisory powers to come up with procedural rules in the absence of congressional direction, then *Miranda* would have to fall in the face of section 3501. This would mean the sixty cases on *Miranda* issues that had been decided by the Supreme Court in the thirty-four years since *Miranda* was handed down would become meaningless. But if the Court decided that *Miranda* was in fact constitutionally required, then how could it explain the systematic chipping away of the decision in all of the cases carving out exceptions—not to mention all of the troublesome language that the Court had used over the years in narrowing the application of *Miranda*? Chief Justice Rehnquist had also shown himself to be one of *Miranda*'s biggest detractors on the bench over the years. What was the Court to do?

With Chief Justice Rehnquist writing the opinion for the seven-member majority, the Supreme Court held that *Miranda* was a constitutional decision of the Court and could not be overruled by an Act of Congress. He also wrote that the Court declined to overrule *Miranda*.[8]

In doing so, the Court disagreed with the conclusion of the Court of Appeals that because of the exceptions created to the application of the *Miranda* warnings, the warnings were not constitutionally required. However, the Court admitted "there is language in some of our opinions that supports the view taken by that court."[9]

The Court relied on several factors in finding *Miranda* to be constitutionally required. First, it noted that *Miranda* and two of its companion cases were in fact state court prosecutions, and that *Miranda* had been historically applied to proceedings arising in state courts. Since the Court has no supervisory power to make procedural rules in state courts, it followed that any intervention would have had to be in a constitutional context.[10] Next, the majority noted many references from the *Miranda* decision itself in which the Court explicitly spoke of providing "constitutional guidelines" for law enforcement and the courts to follow, and meeting "constitutional standards" for the protection of the Fifth Amendment privilege against self-incrimination.[11]

The Court likewise dispensed with the argument that the exceptions to *Miranda* affected its constitutional status. It asserted:

> These decisions illustrate the principle—not that *Miranda* is not a constitutional rule—but that no constitutional rule is immutable. No court laying down a general rule can possibly foresee the various circumstances in which counsel will seek to apply it, and the sort of modifications represented by these cases are as much a normal part of constitutional law as the original decision.[12]

While the Court acknowledged that more remedies existed to correct police misconduct than were available when *Miranda* was decided, it still contended that such remedies, coupled with section 3501, did not meet the "constitutional minimum" that was outlined in *Miranda*.[13]

With regard to its decision not to overrule *Miranda* itself, the majority noted that it did not need to consider whether it would agree with "*Miranda*'s reasoning and its resulting rule" if it were being addressed for the first time, but that the "principles of *stare decisis* weigh heavily against overruling it now."[14] (*Stare decisis*, which is Latin for "to stand by things decided" is the legal concept that states that common law courts should follow previously decided cases as much as possible.) The Court further stated that the fact that *Miranda* had become "embedded in routine police practice to the point where the warnings have become part of our national culture" was another justification for not overruling it.[15] Rather than having watered down *Miranda* through the years, the *Dickerson* majority seemed to suggest that the decision had been finely honed by stating, "If anything, our subsequent cases have reduced the impact of the *Miranda* rule on legitimate law enforcement while reaffirming the decision's core ruling that unwarned statements may not be used as evidence" by the government to help prove its case against the defendant.[16] While admitting that guilty defendants may go free when they invoke their *Miranda* rights, the Court stated that section 3501, and the totality-of-circumstances test that it sought to revive, would be even more troublesome for the police and courts to administer consistently.[17] Finally, the Court noted that while *Miranda* did not "dispense with the voluntariness inquiry" it would be a "rare" case to find statements compelled where the police had abided by the dictates of *Miranda*.[18]

Not all members of the Supreme Court agreed with the decision in *Dickerson*. Justice Antonin Scalia wrote a scathing dissent that was joined by Justice Clarence Thomas. In his dissent, Justice Scalia relied upon the string of cases that had carved out exceptions to *Miranda* over the years as clear evidence that a violation of *Miranda* was not the same thing as a constitutional violation. He stated that while the majority tried to downplay the importance of post-*Miranda* cases, in reality, "the proposition that failure to comply with *Miranda*'s rules does not establish a constitutional violation was central to the holdings of *Tucker, Hass, Quarles*, and *Elstad*."[19] Scalia was angered by what he saw as a lack of logic in the Court's decision in *Dickerson*, claiming that if confessions elicited in violation of *Miranda* amount to constitutional violations, then none of the post-*Miranda* cases made any sense at all, because each of those cases is full of language to the contrary. The complete lack of sense that he saw in the Court's decision in *Dickerson* prompted Scalia to liken the

In the decades since the Miranda *decision, issuing the warning has become a routine part of police procedure. It is even referred to as "Mirandizing."*

Court to a "nine-headed Caesar, giving thumbs-up or thumbs-down to whatever outcome, case by case, that suits or offends its collective fancy."[20] Finally, he countered that in light of the fact that "voluntariness remains the *constitutional* standard," he would continue to apply section 3501 unless it were repealed.[21]

The *Dickerson* decision left both the supporters and the opponents of *Miranda* confused and disappointed. The Court had clearly opted for a compromise. As Yale Kamisar points out, this compromise was one that

> "reaffirmed" *Miranda*'s constitutional status (thereby invalidating the federal statute that purported to overrule it), but it preserved all the

qualifications and exceptions the much-criticized case had acquired over three decades.[22]

But why would Chief Justice Rehnquist have become the late-day champion of *Miranda* after decades of criticism? Kamisar suggests several reasons. First, Rehnquist may have thought that overturning *Miranda* in the year 2000 would have caused more problems than it would have solved. It would have necessitated disposing of thirty years' worth of case law—amounting to sixty cases on *Miranda* issues—that had been decided since *Miranda* was handed down. Also, what would be the point of actually getting rid of *Miranda* when it had been so weakened with the exceptions anyway? It would have caused confusion for both the police and courts if they had to return to the vagaries of the voluntariness test. Whereas as *Miranda* currently stood, once a warning was properly given and, in the majority of cases, waived, a finding that a defendant's statements were compelled was a rare occurrence. Finally, Kamisar notes that the decision in *Dickerson* may have been an admonition to Congress saying, in effect, "Stay off our turf!"[23]

The question remained however: what would be the future of *Miranda* in light of *Dickerson*? For all of the furor caused by the case, perhaps little has changed for the future of *Miranda* in the long run.

chapter 8

Where We Stand Today

How has the Supreme Court dealt with *Miranda* cases in the years since *Dickerson* was decided? Yale Kamisar answers the question by stating, "The hard truth is that in those five years the reaffirmation of *Miranda*'s constitutional status has become less and less meaningful."[1] In reviewing the cases that have come down since *Dickerson*, Kamisar points out that the Court continues to characterize *Miranda* as a "prophylactic rule" (a court-made rule enacted to protect a constitutional right) despite the fact that in *Dickerson* the Court reaffirmed that *Miranda* was a "constitutional decision" of the Court.

Several Supreme Court cases illustrate this. In the case of *Patane* v. *United States*, a detective questioned Samuel Patane about the location of a gun that he supposedly owned without reading him his full set of *Miranda* rights. In response, Patane told the detective where the gun was. Though the prosecution admitted that Patane's statement disclosing the location of the gun was not allowable as evidence in court, it argued that the gun itself should be allowed in as evidence. A unanimous panel for the Tenth Circuit disagreed. Writing for the Tenth Circuit, Judge David Ebel reasoned that *Tucker* and *Elstad*, the cases the government relied upon, were no longer good law since both cases "were predicated upon the premise that the *Miranda* rule was a prophylactic rule, rather than a constitutional rule."[2] Since the "poisonous tree" doctrine requires suppression of the fruits (or evidence) that arises from unconstitutional conduct, the court found the suppression of the gun to be required.

The Supreme Court, however, disagreed. Despite the fact that the Court did not refer to the *Miranda* rules as "prophylactic" in *Dickerson*, Justice Clarence Thomas, whose opinion was joined by Justice Antonin Scalia and Chief Justice William Rehnquist, harken back to this language, and continually refer to the *Miranda* warnings as "prophylactic."[3] Relying on language from *Elstad*, Justice Thomas reiterated that the *Miranda* rules are broader than and "necessarily sweep" beyond the protections of the Self-Incrimination Clause. Indeed, Thomas specifically stated that simply failing to give a suspect his *Miranda* warnings did not, by itself, violate a suspect's constitutional rights, and that the Court followed this view since *Dickerson* had been decided.[4] In his concurring opinion, Justice Anthony M. Kennedy likewise did not rely on *Dickerson* but rather cited with approval the language in *Elstad* that spoke of cases that allowed evidence after a *Miranda* failure as "based in large part on our recognition that the concerns underlying the *Miranda* rule must be accommodated to other objectives of the criminal justice system."[5] Kennedy is saying that concern for a suspect's rights must be balanced against other goals of law enforcement, which in this case is the important value of reliable physical evidence.

In *Missouri* v. *Seibert*, the Court again made its decision without relying on *Dickerson*. In that case, the police used what has become a notorious tactic to get around the *Miranda* requirements. The police officer questioned the suspect informally, and the defendant confessed. The police officer then stopped the questioning, took a short break, and then read the *Miranda* warnings to the suspect and asked her to again make her confession, this time on tape. The Court did not stand for the use of two-stage interrogation technique.

Justice David H. Souter, writing for a 5–4 majority, noted that while in *Elstad* the *Miranda* failure was inadvertent, in *Seibert* the police officer made a "conscious decision" to withhold the *Miranda* warnings. Basically, the Court was not going to stand for a "police strategy adapted to undermine the *Miranda* warnings."[6] The Court held:

> Because the question-first tactic effectively threatens to thwart *Miranda*'s purpose of reducing the risk that a coerced confession would be admitted, and because the facts here do not reasonably support a conclusion that the warnings given could have served their purpose, Seibert's postwarning statements are inadmissible.[7]

While this appears to be a victory for *Miranda*, Yale Kamisar aptly points out that "the failure to comply with *Miranda* was so deliberate and so flagrant that an 8–1 or 7–2 ruling in favor of the defense would not have been surprising. The fact that the vote on these extreme facts was 5–4 . . . is significant evidence of the low state to which *Miranda* has fallen."[8]

In light of the decisions in *Patane* and *Seibert*, Kamisar asks whether *Dickerson* accomplished anything, other than to invalidate section 3501. The answer seems to be no. *Dickerson* seems to have completed the exceptions carved out in *Tucker*, *Quarles*, and *Elstad*. Kamisar also points out that, because of his "flipflop[ping]" stances in key *Miranda* cases, Chief Justice Rehnquist perhaps "contributed more to the confusion over *Miranda* than any other member of the Court."[9]

In another recent case, *Yarborough* v. *Alvarado*, the Supreme Court was asked to rule on the part of *Miranda* that dealt with a suspect's being in custody. In that case, Michael Alvarado, a seventeen-year-old student, was suspected in connection with a murder and robbery. A detective contacted Alvarado's mother about bringing him in for an interview. When his parents brought him in, he was questioned by a police officer for two hours without receiving his *Miranda* warnings. After the interview, Alvarado was not arrested, and he was allowed to leave with his parents. Later Alvarado was charged with second-degree murder and attempted robbery. Alvarado's attorney moved to suppress the statements in the interview on the grounds that his Fifth and Sixth Amendment rights had been violated. The trial court denied his motion to suppress his interview statements on *Miranda* grounds, and Alvarado was convicted.

Following his conviction, Alvarado brought a petition in federal district court against Yarborough, the warden of the prison where he was being held. The district court denied Alvarado's petition. However, the Ninth Circuit Court of Appeals reversed the decision holding that Alvarado was in custody when he was interrogated by police and, therefore, should have been read his *Miranda* warnings. The Ninth Circuit reasoned that the state court erred in failing to take into consideration Alvarado's youth and inexperience when determining whether a reasonable person in his position would have felt that he was free to leave the interview.

The Supreme Court reversed this decision. In an opinion by Justice Kennedy, the Court found that the state court had considered the proper factors and reached a reasonable conclusion that Alvarado was not in custody for *Miranda* purposes during his police interview.[10] The Court further stated that its decisions in custody cases never indicated that age or experience had to be taken into consideration. The Court was not persuaded by the fact that Alvarado had no prior experience with law enforcement and may not have known that he was free to leave, since no one expressly told him. The Court stated that police officers did not have to consider such factors when deciding when suspects should be advised of their *Miranda* rights.[11]

With its rulings in the cases since *Dickerson*, the Court seems to be sending a clear signal that *Dickerson* will be more or less ignored, and that it will continue to give *Miranda* a narrow interpretation.

The Future of *Miranda* v. *Arizona*

Miranda v. *Arizona* has been called the best-known criminal justice decision, and perhaps the best-known legal decision, in all of American history.[12] In spite of all the controversy it has ignited, there is little doubt that *Miranda* has had a long-term impact on several key areas of the criminal justice system. *Miranda* scholar Richard Leo has written of four areas where he believes *Miranda* has had a lasting impact. First, *Miranda* has increased the professionalism of police officers and is responsible for stamping out the last remains of the notorious "third degree." Next, *Miranda* has affected how the police think about and approach the process of custodial interrogation. Third, *Miranda* has increased the public's awareness of constitutional rights. Finally, *Miranda* has challenged the police to come up with what Leo refers to as "more specialized, more sophisticated, and seemingly more effective inter-rogation techniques" to use with suspects to extract damaging statements during custodial interrogation.[13]

Despite *Miranda*'s impact on the criminal justice system, it seems clear that the Warren Court's objec-tives in devising the *Miranda* warnings have *not* been met in the decades since the case was decided. Leo argues: "If the goal of *Miranda* was to reduce the kinds of interrogation techniques and custodial pressures that create stationhouse compulsion and coercion, then it appears to have failed miserably."[14] Rather, Leo suggests:

> The reading of rights and the taking of waivers has become, seemingly, an empty ritual, and American police continue to use the same psychological methods of persuasion, manipulation, and deception that the Warren Court roundly criticized in *Miranda*.[15]

Leo asserts that as society moves into twenty-first century, *Miranda*'s impact will be slight. It seems that over the course of the past four decades,

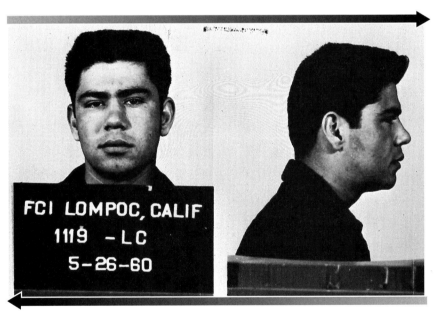

These mug shots were taken of Ernesto Miranda after an arrest that took place before the kidnapping and rape of Lois Ann Jameson. Despite continuing arguments over whether the Miranda *decision should stand, the case has had an enormous impact on the American legal system.*

all of the players in the criminal justice system—the police, prosecutors, and courts—have each "adapted to and diluted *Miranda*, using it to advance their own bureaucratic objectives rather than to meaningfully enforce the privilege against self-incrimination or the right to counsel."[16] Leo maintains that the police have learned to "sidestep" *Miranda* or employ "clever strategies" to elicit a high number of waivers, while prosecutors have become adept at using *Miranda* to aid in the admission of confession evidence, assist in plea bargaining, and support cases at trial.[17] Finally, courts' reliance on *Miranda* has shifted the inquiry so that the focus is not on whether a confession was voluntary but on whether *Miranda* protocol was followed.[18]

Leo further maintains that *Miranda* has become a "low-cost proposition," meaning that it places only a small burden on the various players in the criminal justice system. Contrary to the arguments of opponents like Paul Cassell, Leo says that since "there is no compelling evidence that *Miranda* causes a significant number of lost convictions . . . the best evidence suggests that this difficult-to-ascertain figure is likely to be very low."[19] The other side of the coin is that while *Miranda* is a low-cost proposition to maintain, it ultimately offers few benefits to those it was designed to protect. *Miranda* simply has not changed the "psychological interrogation process" that the Warren Court was so mindful of in crafting its decision in *Miranda*, Leo says, if anything, the combination of "more subtle and sophisticated" interrogation strategies have only increased the inherent compulsion present in the interrogation room.[20]

If *Miranda* is likely to play a limited role in protecting suspects into the twenty-first century, then what can be done to fill in the gaps left by *Miranda*? Leo and other scholars look to electronic audio or video recording of interrogation room proceedings as "the most promising interrogation reform of our era."[21] The biggest benefit of video recording interrogations is that it "creates an objective, comprehensive, and reviewable record of the interrogation for all parties."[22] Having a videotaped record reduces the "swearing contest" aspect of a trial where the police swear to one version of what happened during the interrogation while the defendant swears to a very different version of events. This, in turn, reduces court costs and valuable court time in trying to ascertain which version of events is the truth. Videotaping would likewise be a benefit to all parties in that the recording "deters false allegations of [police] impropriety just as it deters police misconduct inside the interrogation room."[23]

Other experts agree that the time is now for videotaped interrogations. Margaret Talbot, Senior

Fellow at the New America Foundation, writes that "in the era of amateur videos, Court TV, and twenty-four-hour-a-day news coverage, we have come to expect a video record of almost anything that matters to law or to history, and plenty of things that don't."[24] Talbot points to police departments such as those in San Diego and Kansas City, where the police videotape interrogation proceedings voluntarily, and to those in Minnesota and Alaska, which are required to do so under law. Though some of the police officers were skeptical at first, according to a 1993 Justice Department study of police videotaping, which is the most comprehensive data available, 97 percent of the departments that tape these proceedings find it "very useful" or "somewhat useful."[25] It has been called "a powerful truth-finding tool" and described as being "in the same category as DNA evidence."[26]

Professor Kenneth Haas of the University of Delaware agrees with the wisdom of videotaping all station house police interrogations. He states:

> Such a requirement, enforced over time and with the bugs worked out, probably would do a lot more to curb coerced confessions and reduce wrongful convictions than the largely illusionary good effects of what is left of the *Miranda* rule. It would also reduce the number of cases in which a truly guilty defendant benefits from a factually incorrect ruling that a confession was improperly obtained.[27]

Haas has called videotaping "one of those rare innovations that can help either side in the criminal-justice system, for the simple reason that it serves the quest to find out what really happened . . . the quest for the truth."[28] The problem, however, may be in persuading police departments that are not currently videotaping interrogations that undertaking the costs and training involved to institute such a program would be to their benefit in the long run.

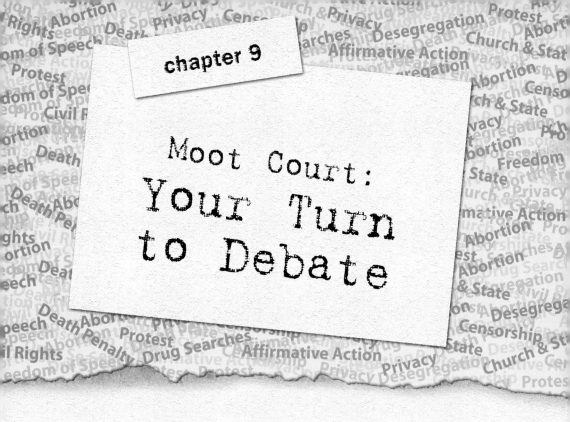

chapter 9

Moot Court: Your Turn to Debate

A mock judicial proceeding is a fun way to get a "hands on" feel for how a real court case occurs. Taking part can help students better understand what is involved in a real court case. There is much more to it than what is shown on TV or in the movies.

One type of judicial exercise is called "moot court." Moot court is a staging of a hypothetical or fictitious case or a real case that went before an appeals court or the Supreme Court. The purpose of these courts is to rule on a lower court's decision. It differs from a trial in that no witnesses appear and testify, just as no witnesses are called in a Supreme Court case. The focus of the case is whether the lower court erred, or made mistakes, rather than determining all the facts of the case.

In moot court, the players take the roles of judges, clerks, attorneys, and journalists. They do research, write briefs, and argue legal issues before a mock panel of appeals court judges. The exercise sharpens players' research, writing, and debating skills.

Participating in a moot court activity is a fun way to see how real court cases occur and proceed. Here's how to try a moot court activity with your own class or club.[1]

Step 1: Assign Roles

Here are the roles you will need to fill:

1. Nine justices. Choose one person to act as the Chief Justice and direct the proceeding. The justices will hear the attorneys' arguments, question them, and then write and deliver the final ruling. The court's majority opinion is the position agreed upon by a majority of the judges. Individual judges may choose to issue a concurring or dissenting opinion in the case.

2. Two or more court clerks. The clerks work with the judges to prepare at least five questions to ask the attorneys during oral arguments. The clerks also help with research for the judges' opinions.

3. A team of two or more attorneys for the appellant (the party asking the court to reverse the lower court decision).

4. A team of two or more attorneys for the appellee (the party that won the lower court decision and asks that the decision stand as it is).

5. Each team has a designated spokesperson to present the argument, but any of the attorneys can answer questions from the judges. Attorneys must address the major issues by presenting the most persuasive arguments for their side.

6. Two or more reporters. The reporters interview the attorneys and write news stories about the facts of the case and the final ruling.

7. The bailiff, who calls the court to order.

Step 2: Prepare Your Case

Part 1: Gather Information

The participants should become familiar with the following cases:

◇ *Miranda* v. *Arizona*

◇ *Michigan* v. *Tucker*

◇ *New York* v. *Quarles*

◇ *Oregon* v. *Elstad*

◇ *Dickerson* v. *United States*

See chapters 3, 6, and 7 for the basic facts on these cases. More detailed information, such as court opinions, are available on the Internet. Another source of information is experts from your community, such as the following:

◇ An attorney who specializes in criminal defense work.

◇ A professor of criminal justice from a local college.

◇ An advocacy group. Representatives from victims' rights groups or law enforcement organizations may agree to discuss their group's point of view on the case.

You will be arguing the Supreme Court case of *Dickerson* v. *United States*, in which the Supreme Court decided that *Miranda* v. *Arizona* was a constitutional decision of the Court and could not be overturned by an act of Congress. (See chapter 7 for more information on the case.) Students may want to consider the following questions when compiling their arguments and preparing their questions:

1. What are the arguments in favor of *Miranda* v. *Arizona* being held as a constitutional decision of the Court?

2. What does the Court mean when it refers to the *Miranda* warnings as being "prophylactic" in nature?

3. If the *Miranda* warnings are constitutionally required, how can the Court reconcile the cases in which exceptions to *Miranda* have been carved out?

4. How does 18 U.S.C. section 3501, the statute at issue in *Dickerson*, differ from what the Warren Court prescribed in *Miranda v. Arizona*?

Part 2: Write Your Briefs

A legal brief is a written presentation of your argument. Brainstorm with the lawyers on your team. Which arguments are strongest for you? What are your weaknesses?

You may want to divide up arguments for research and writing. If so, be sure to work as a team to put the brief together. Otherwise, your brief may have weak points or be difficult to read.

The cover page should have the case name, *United States* v. *Dickerson*, and should state whether it is the case for the appellant or appellee. It should also list the attorneys' names.

The text of the brief should have the following sections:

A. Statement of the issue for review: What is the question before the Court?

B. Statement of the case: What is this case about? How did the trial court rule?

C. Statement of the facts: Briefly describe the facts relevant to the case.

D. Summary of the argument: Sum up your argument in 150 words or less.

E. Argument: Spell out the legal arguments that support your side. You can split this into sections with subheadings for each part. Include references to cases or authorities that support your side.

F. Conclusion: Ask the court to rule for your client.

Real briefs may be thirty pages long. Limit your brief to no more than five typed pages, double-spaced, or about 1,250 words. If possible, type on a computer. Otherwise, write very neatly.

On an agreed-upon date, each team gives the other side a copy of its brief. Each judge gets a copy too. If you do this in class, then give the teacher a copy. Be sure each team member keeps a copy of the brief.

In real life, lawyers often prepare reply briefs, which answer points made by the other side. You will not do that, but you should be ready to answer their points in oral argument.

Part 3: Prepare for Oral Argument

Judges should read all the briefs before the oral argument. They should prepare questions for the lawyers. Each side will have up to fifteen minutes to argue its case. Run through your arguments out loud and be ready to be interrupted with questions.

Step 3: Hold the Oral Argument

Part 1: Assemble the Participants

◇ The judges sit in a panel at the head of the room. They should not enter until the bailiff calls the court to order. A speaking podium faces the bench.

◇ The appellant's team of attorneys sits on one side, facing the judges.

◇ The appellee's team sits on the opposite side, also facing the judges.

◇ The reporters sit at the back.

◇ As the judges enter, the bailiff calls the court to order: "Oyez (oy-yay)! Oyez! Oyez! The Supreme Court of the United States is now in session with the Honorable Chief Justice _____ presiding. All will stand and remain standing until the judges are seated and the Chief Justice has asked all present to be seated." ("Oyez" means "Hear ye.")

Part 2: Present the Case

◇ The Chief Justice calls the case and asks whether the parties are ready. Each team's spokesperson answers, "Yes."

◇ The appellant's spokesperson approaches the podium saying, "May it please the Court," and then begins the team's argument. Judges may interrupt when they wish to ask a question. The attorneys should respectfully answer any questions as asked. Do not get flustered if a judge interrupts with a question, and do not attempt to speak over the judges. Answer the question honestly and then move on. The appellee's spokesperson presents his or her team's arguments in the same way.

◇ Each team has up to fifteen minutes to present its argument. If the appellant's team wants, it can save five minutes of its time to rebut the appellee's argument. If so, the spokesperson should inform the Court before sitting down.

◇ After the arguments, the bailiff asks every-one to rise as the judges retire to chambers to debate their decision.

◇ At this time, reporters may interview lawyers for the parties and begin working on their articles.

Step 4: Publish and Report the Decision

A few days later, the Court issues its majority opin-ion in written form, along with any dissenting opinions and individual concurring opinions. Reporters may interview the lawyers again. The reporters' stories discussing the case and the out-come are due the next day. The articles should be five hundred words or less.

Questions for Discussion

1. Why is it important to protect the rights of the accused? Has the Supreme Court gone too far in its efforts to do so?

2. Since suspects usually waive their protections under *Miranda* and go on to speak to and incriminate themselves to the police, what can be done to educate suspects about retaining their rights under *Miranda*?

3. Why do you think the majority of law enforcement organizations actually agree that *Miranda* v. *Arizona* should not be overturned?

4. Suppose you are an attorney and a former client calls you from his house. The police arrived at his front door and asked if they could talk to him about a recent rash of robberies in the area. The client admits to you that he drove a getaway car for one of the robberies but was not involved otherwise. The police are now waiting in his living room. How would you advise this client?

5. What do you think the future of *Miranda* v. *Arizona* is?

Chapter Notes

Introduction

   1. 384 U.S. 436 (1966).

Chapter 1. The Crime and Conviction

   1. As reported in the departmental records of the Phoenix, Arizona, police department.

   2. Liva Baker, *Miranda: Crime, Law, and Politics* (New York: Atheneum, 1983), p. 13.

   3. Ibid.

   4. 378 U.S. 478, 490–491(1964).

Chapter 2. The Rights of the Accused: En Route to *Miranda*

   1. Otis H. Stephens, Jr., *The Supreme Court and Confessions of Guilt* (Knoxville: University of Tennessee Press, 1973), p. 18. See also *The Columbia Encyclopedia,* Sixth Edition, 2001–2005, <http://www.bartleby.com/65/or/ordeal.html> (January 3, 2006).

   2. Ibid., pp. 18–19.

   3. Ibid., p. 19.

   4. *The Columbia Encyclopedia*, Sixth Edition, 2001–2005, <http://www.bartleby.com/65/st/StarCham.html> (January 3, 2006).

   5. Stephens, pp. 19–20.

   6. National Archives and Records Administration, "Bill of Rights," n.d., <http://www.archives.gov/national-archives-experience/charters/bill_of_rights.html> (January 7, 2006).

   7. 32 U.S. 243, 247–248, 250 (1833).

   8. "Notes on the Amendments: 14th Amendment," *The U.S. Constitution Online,* March 15, 2006, <http://www.usconstitution.net/constamnotes.html> (May 24, 2006).

9. 287 U.S. at 71.

10. Ibid.

11. 297 U.S. 278, 285–286 (1936).

12. 297 U.S. at 286.

13. Stephen A. Saltzburg, Daniel J. Capra, Angela J. Davis, eds., *Basic Criminal Procedure,* 3rd edition, Black Letter Series (St. Paul, Minn.: West Group, 2003), p. 375.

14. Ibid., p. 375.

15. 367 U.S. 643, 644 (1961).

16. 372 U.S. 335 (1963).

17. *Betts* v. *Brady*, 316 U.S. 455 (1942).

18. 372 U.S. at 344.

19. 378 U.S. 478, 491 (1964).

20. Stephens, pp. 127–128.

21. Ibid., p. 128.

Chapter 3. The Supreme Court and the *Miranda* Case

1. Supreme Court of the United States, "A Brief Overview of the Supreme Court," "The Court and Constitutional Interpretation," n.d., <http://www.supremecourtus.gov/about/abriefoverview-supreme court.pdf> (January 15, 2006). See also James A. Inciardi, *Criminal Justice* (New York: Harcourt Brace Jovanovich, 1987), pp. 376–377.

2. Supreme Court of the United States, "The Justices' Caseload," n.d., <http://www.supremecourtus.gov/about/justicecaseload.pdf> (January 15, 2006).

3. Supreme Court of the United States, "The Court and its Procedures," n.d., <http://www.supremecourtus.gov/about/procedures.pdf> (January 15, 2006).

4. Otis H. Stephens, Jr., *The Supreme Court and Confessions of Guilt* (Knoxville: University of Tennessee Press, 1973), p. 129.

5. "Not Just Any Court: The Supreme Court and *Miranda* v. *Arizona*," *exploredc.org*, n.d., <http://www.exploredc.org/pdfs/supremecourt.pdf> (January 15, 2006).

6. Peter Irons and Stephanie Guitton, eds., *May It Please the Court* (New York: The New Press, 1993), p. 217.

7. Ibid.

8. Ibid., p. 218.

9. Ibid., p. 219.

10. Ibid., p. 220.

11. Ibid., pp. 221–222.

12. 384 U.S. at 444.

13. 384 U.S. at 478–479.

14. 384 U.S. at 449–455.

15. 384 U.S. at 455.

16. 384 U.S. at 457.

17. 384 U.S. at 458.

18. Stephen A. Saltzburg, Daniel J. Capra, Angela J. Davis, eds., *Basic Criminal Procedure*, 3rd edition, Black Letter Series (St. Paul, Minn.: West Group, 2003), p. 385.

19. 384 U.S. at 467.

20. 384 U.S. at 491.

21. 384 U.S. at 503.

22. 384 U.S. at 517.

23. 384 U.S. at 533–534, 545.

24. 384 U.S. at 537.

25. 384 U.S. at 542–543.

26. Stephens, p. 129.

27. Robert F. Cushman, *Cases in Constitutional Law* (Englewood Cliffs, N.J.: Prentice-Hall, 1979), p. 400.

Chapter 4. In the Wake of *Miranda*: Arguments in Favor of the *Miranda* Warnings

1. Hollida Wakefield and Ralph Underwager, "Coerced or Nonvoluntary Confessions," *Institute for Psychological Therapies,* March 8, 2006 <http://www.ipt-forensics.com/library/coerced.htm> (February 17, 2005), p. 1.

2. "Miranda Rights," Office of the Public Defender, 20th Judicial Circuit, State of Florida, n.d., <http://public defender.cjis20.org/miranda.htm> (April 20, 2006).

3. Wakefield and Underwager, pp. 1–2.

4. Ibid., p. 6.

5. Ibid.

6. Ibid.

7. Ibid., p. 3.

8. Ibid.

9. Ibid., p. 6.

10. "Milgram Basics," *StanleyMilgram.com,* n.d. <http://www.stanleymilgram.com/milgram.php> (January 21, 2006).

11. Wakefield and Underwager, p. 7.

12. "Miranda Rights," *NewsHour with Jim Lehrer* transcript, January 6, 2000, <http://www.pbs.org/newshour/bb/law/jan-june00/miranda_1-6.html> (December 11, 2004), p. 2.

13. Ibid., p. 3.

14. "Reconsidering Miranda," *NewsHour with Jim Lehrer* transcript, April 19, 2000, <http://www.pbs.org/newshour/bb/law/jan-jun00/miranda_4-19.html> (August 2, 2005), p. 2.

15. Ibid., p. 4.

16. Ibid.

17. Kris Axtman, "The *Miranda* Rule: The Tale Behind Cops' Most Famous Words," *Christian Science Monitor,* Vol. 92, Issue 10, April 14, 2000.

18. Ibid.

19. Welsh S. White, "Defending *Miranda*: A Reply to Professor Caplan," 39 Vand.L.Rev. (1986) p. 17.

20. Ibid.

21. Ibid.

22. Ibid., p. 18.

23. Ibid.

24. Peter Irons and Stephanie Guitton, eds., *May It Please the Court* (New York: The New Press, 1993), p. 222; Axtman.

25. "Miranda Rights," p. 5.

26. White, p. 22.

27. "Miranda Rights," p. 5.

Chapter 5. In the Wake of *Miranda*: Arguments Against the *Miranda* Warnings

1. Paul G. Cassell, "*Miranda*'s Social Costs: An Empirical Reassessment," in *The Miranda Debate: Law, Justice, and Policing*, eds. Richard A. Leo and George C. Thomas III (Boston: Northeastern University Press, 1998), p. 176.

2. Ibid., pp. 178–179.

3. Ibid., pp. 179–181.

4. Ibid., p. 181.

5. Ibid., p. 183.

6. Ibid., pp. 183–184

7. Ibid., 185.

8. Stephen J. Schulhofer, "*Miranda, Dickerson*, and the Puzzling Persistence of Fifth Amendment Exceptionalism," Michigan Law Review Symposium, "*Miranda* After *Dickerson*: The Future of Confession Law," March 2001, Vol. 99, No. 5, p. 943.

9. D. Kyle Sampson, "The Technical Reality: Rules for Questioning Suspects Have Become Constitutional Straightjackets," posted by Dr. Coleman McGinnis, under title "Two Views of *Miranda*," March 1999, <http://

www.tnstate.edu/cmcginnis/twoviewsofmiranda.htm>
(October 10, 2004).

10. Gerald M. Caplan, "Questioning *Miranda*," in *The
Miranda Debate: Law, Justice, and Policing*, eds. Richard
A. Leo and George C. Thomas III (Boston: Northeastern
University Press, 1998), pp. 127–128.

11. Ibid., pp. 129–130.

12. Ibid., p. 130.

13. Kenneth Haas, University of Delaware, e-mail
message to author, June 27, 2005.

14. Ibid.

15. Ibid.

16. Richard A. Leo, "Miranda and the Problem of False
Confessions," in *The Miranda Debate: Law, Justice, and
Policing*, eds. Richard A. Leo and George C. Thomas III
(Boston: Northeastern University Press, 1989), p. 275.

17. George C. Thomas, "Missing *Miranda*'s Story, A
Review of Gary L. Stuart's *Miranda: The Story of America's
Right to Remain Silent*," (Newark, N.J.: Rutgers Law
School Faculty Papers, 2005), p. 686.

18. David Simon, "Homicide: A Year on the Killing
Streets," in *The Miranda Debate: Law, Justice, and
Policing*, eds. Richard A. Leo and George C. Thomas III
(Boston: Northeastern University Press, 1998), p. 56.

19. Thomas, p. 686.

20. Simon, pp. 59–60.

21. Leo, p. 271.

22. Ibid., p. 275.

23. Ibid.

24. Ibid., pp. 275–276.

25. Ibid.

26. Ibid., pp. 276–277.

27. Caplan, p. 122.

28. Ibid., p. 123.

29. Harold J. Rothwax, *Guilty: The Collapse of Criminal Justice* (New York: Random House, 1996), p. 80.

30. Ibid., pp. 80–81.

31. Ibid., p. 81.

Chapter 6. The Progeny of *Miranda*: The Court Chips Away

1. 401 U.S. 222, 225 (1971).
2. 417 U.S. 433, 443–446 (1974).
3. 417 U.S. at 443, 445.
4. 420 U.S. 714 (1975).
5. 420 U.S. at 723.
6. 420 U.S. at 725.
7. 467 U.S. 649, 651 (1984).
8. 467 U.S. at 653, 658.
9. 470 U.S. 298, 307 (1985).
10. 470 U.S. at 318.
11. 470 U.S. at 319.
12. Yale Kamisar, "*Dickerson* v. *United States*: The Case That Disappointed *Miranda*'s Critics—and Then Its Supporters," University of San Diego School of Law, Public Law and Legal Theory Research Paper Series, Paper 33, 2005, p. 27.
13. Yale Kamisar, "Foreword: From *Miranda* to Section 3501 to *Dickerson* to . . ." Michigan Law Review Symposium, "*Miranda* After *Dickerson*: The Future of Confession Law," March 2001, Vol. 99, No. 5, p. 879.

Chapter 7. *Dickerson v. United States*: Clarity or More Confusion?

1. Yale Kamisar, "Foreword: From *Miranda* to 3501 to *Dickerson* to . . ." Michigan Law Review Symposium, "*Miranda* After *Dickerson*: The Future of Confession Law," March 2001, Vol. 99, No. 5, pp. 879–880.
2. Ibid., p. 882.

3. Ibid., p. 881.

4. Yale Kamisar, Wayne R. LaFave, and Jerold H. Israel, eds., *Basic Criminal Procedure*, 6th edition, American Casebook Series (St. Paul, Minn.: West Publishing Co., 1986), p. 573.

5. "Miranda Rights," *NewsHour with Jim Lehrer* transcript, January 6, 2000, <http://www.pbs.org/newshour/bb/law/jan-june00/miranda_1-6.html> (December 11, 2004), p. 5.

6. Kamisar, LaFave, and Israel, p. 392.

7. 530 U.S. 428, 432 (2000).

8. Ibid.

9. 530 U.S. at 438.

10. Ibid.

11. 530 U.S. at 439.

12. 530 U.S. at 441.

13. 530 U.S. at 442.

14. 530 U.S. at 443.

15. Ibid.

16. 530 U.S. at 443, 444.

17. 530 U.S. at 444.

18. Ibid.

19. 530 U.S. at 454.

20. 530 U.S. at 455.

21. 530 U.S. at 465.

22. Kamisar, p. 889.

23. Ibid., pp. 890–892.

Chapter 8. Where We Stand Today

1. Yale Kamisar, "*Dickerson* v. *United States*: The Case That Disappointed *Miranda*'s Critics—and Then Its Supporters," University of San Diego School of Law, Public Law and Legal Theory Research Paper Series, Paper 33, 2005, p. 1.

2. *Patane* v. *United States*, 304 F.3d 1013, 1019 (10th Cir. 2002) (Ebel, J.,) rev'd, 124 S.Ct. 2620 (2004).

3. 124 S.Ct. 2620, 2626–2627, 2630 (2004).

4. 124 S.Ct. at 2627, 2622.

5. 124 S.Ct. at 2631.

6. 124 S.Ct. 2601, 2606, 2612 (2004).

7. 124 S.Ct. at 2613.

8. Kamisar, p. 43.

9. Ibid., p. 45.

10. 124 S.Ct. 2140, 2150 (2004).

11. 124 S.Ct. at 2151, 2152.

12. Richard Leo, "Questioning the Relevance of *Miranda* in the Twenty-First Century," Michigan Law Review Symposium, "*Miranda* After *Dickerson*: The Future of Confession Law," March 2001, Vol. 99, No. 5, p. 1000.

13. Ibid., p. 1026.

14. Ibid., p. 1021.

15. Ibid.

16. Ibid., pp. 1026–1027.

17. Ibid., p. 1027.

18. Ibid.

19. Ibid., p. 1027.

20. Ibid.

21. Ibid., p. 1028.

22. Ibid.

23. Ibid.

24. Margaret Talbot, "True Confessions," *The Atlantic Monthly*, July 1, 2002, New American Foundation, <http///www.newamerica.net/index.cfm?pg=article&DocID =875> (February 17, 2005).

25. Ibid.

26. Ibid.

27. Kenneth Haas, University of Delaware, e-mail message to author, June 27, 2005.

28. Ibid.

Chapter 9. Moot Court: Your Turn to Debate

1. Adapted from Millie Aulbur, "Constitutional Issues and Teenagers," *The Missouri Bar*, n.d., <http://www.mobar.org/teach/clesson.htm> (December 10, 2004); Street Law, Inc., and The Supreme Court Historical Society, "Moot Court Activity," 2002, <http://www.land markcases.org/mootcourt.html> (December 10, 2004); with suggestions from Ron Fridell and Kathiann M. Kowalski.

* * *

Illustration Credits: Arizona State Library, Archives and Public Records, History and Archives Division, pp. 10, 98; Fabian Bachrach/Collection of the Supreme Court of the United States, p. 40; Digital Stock, p. 89; Hemera Image Express, p. 2; Library of Congress, p. 22; RG107, Maricopa County, SG 8, Superior Court 1963-1071, Phoenix AZ: Arizona State Archives, Department of Library, Archives, and Public Records, p. 77.

Cover Illustrations: Artville (background); Arizona State Library, Archives and Public Records, History and Archives Division (photograph).

Glossary

admissibility—Whether or not information or evidence will be allowed to be heard in court. The judge determines what evidence will be admissible at trial.

bright-line rule—A judicial rule that tends to resolve ambiguous legal issues in a simple and straightforward matter, though sometimes sacrificing fairness for certainty.

capital case—A case in which execution is a possible punishment.

common law—System of law based on judicial decisions, customs, and traditions rather than on statutes and codes.

due process of law—Legal concept introduced into American law in the Fifth and Fourteenth Amendments to the United States Constitution. It stands for the principle that the government may not deprive an individual of life, liberty, or property unless certain legal rules and procedures are followed. The concept asserts fundamental principles of justice and guarantees that laws do not violate private rights of the individual.

evidence—Refers to things brought into court regarding a case. Evidence can include testimony, documents, and physical objects, such as weapons or contraband, that tend to prove or disprove an alleged fact in a case.

felony—An offense punishable by one year or more of imprisonment.

fruits of the poisonous tree—Doctrine in criminal procedure that states that evidence resulting from an illegal search, arrest, or interrogation is inadmissible in court because the evidence was tainted by the illegality.

impeachment—The act of discrediting a witness, such as in proving that a witness made prior inconsistent statements.

incorporation doctrine—The process of applying most of the amendments in the Bill of Rights to the states by interpreting the Fourteenth Amendment's Due Process clause as including these provisions.

interrogation—The formal questioning of a person by the police; usually of a person arrested for or suspected of committing a crime. **Custodial interrogation** refers to questioning initiated by police after a person has been taken into custody or otherwise deprived of his freedom in any significant way.

jurisdiction—Refers to a court or judge's power to make judicial decisions; the territory in which a specific court can exercise its authority.

lineup—A police procedure in which a criminal suspect and others who are physically similar are shown to the victim or witness to determine whether the suspect can be identified as the one who committed the crime.

misdemeanor—A crime that is less serious than a felony and is usually punishable by less severe penalties.

plea bargain—An agreement between a criminal defendant and the prosecutor in which the defendant agrees to plead guilty to a lesser crime in exchange for a more lenient punishment after conviction.

prophylactic rules—Safeguards created by courts that reinforce rights protected by the Constitution but are not constitutional rights in and of themselves.

stare decisis—Latin for "to stand by things decided." Refers to the principle that common law courts follow previously decided cases as much as possible.

waiver—The knowing and voluntary relinquishment—either express or implied—of a legal right.

Further Reading

Books

Campbell, Andrea. *Rights of the Accused*. Philadelphia: Chelsea House Publishers, 2001.

Compston, Christine L. *Earl Warren: Justice for All*. Oxford and New York: Oxford University Press, 2001.

Fridell, Ron. *Miranda Law: The Right to Remain Silent*. New York: Marshall Cavendish, 2005.

Sonneborn, Liz. *Miranda v. Arizona*. New York: The Rosen Publishing Group, Inc., 2004.

Wormser, Richard. *Defending the Accused: Stories from the Courtroom*. New York: Franklin Watts, 2001.

Internet Addresses

Common Sense Americanism: Miranda v. Arizona

<http://www.csamerican.com/SC.asp?r=384+U.S.+436>

Landmark Supreme Court Cases: Miranda v. Arizona

<http://www.landmarkcases.org/miranda/home.html>

Miranda *v. Arizona*

<http://caselaw.lp.findlaw.com/scripts/getcase.pl?court=US&vol=384&invol=436>

Index

O

O'Connor, Sandra Day, 80
Oregon v. Elstad, 79–81, 88, 92, 93, 94, 105
Oregon v. Hass, 78, 88

P

Patane v. United States, 91–93, 94
petitioner defined, 33
Pittsburgh study, 57
plea-bargaining, 65
police. *See* law enforcement.
Police and Criminal Evidence Act, 64
Powell, Lewis F., 74
Powell v. Alabama, 19–20
precedent defined, 23, 33
property, seizure of, 17, 18, 20, 65
prophylactic rule, 76, 91–92
public safety exception, 78–79

R

Rehnquist, William, 74, 76, 85, 90, 92, 94–95
respondent defined, 33
right against self-incrimination, 15–16, 17, 35, 38, 39, 43, 54, 67, 76, 86, 93. *See also* Fifth Amendment.
right to an attorney. *See also* Sixth Amendment.
in Ernesto Miranda case, 9–12, 35
in interrogations, 9–12, 26–29, 37–39, 72, 78
right to remain silent. *See also* Fifth Amendment.
confessions and, 11, 12, 63, 64
in interrogations, 28, 35, 37–40, 44
statement of, 48
Rothwax, Harold J., 72

S

Scalia, Antonin, 88–89, 92
Scottsboro Nine case, 19–20
search warrant, 25

section 3501. *See* Admissibility of Confessions legislation.
Sixth Amendment, 27–29, 35, 39, 95. *See also* right to an attorney.
Souter, David H., 94
"Sporting Theory" of justice, 71–73
stare decisis, 87
Stewart, Potter, 35, 36
suspects
credibility, impeachment of, 75, 78
rights of, 35–39, 42–45, 49
waiver of rights by, 34, 44, 68, 70–71, 90

T

Talbot, Margaret, 100–101
"third degree," 39
Thomas, Clarence, 88, 92, 93
torture and confessions, 14–16, 20–23
totality-of-circumstances test, 23–24, 43, 88
trial by ordeal, 13–14

U

United States Supreme Court
on the Bill of Rights, 17
decision of, 38–46
described, 30–32
on due process, 18–21, 26–27
Miranda's appeal to, 12, 32, 34–35
on *Miranda* constitutionality, 83–90
Miranda exceptions by, 75–76, 78–81
restructuring of, 74–75

W

Warren, Earl, 36, 37–38, 39–40, 74
White, Byron, 36, 44–45
writ of certiorari defined, 32, 33

Y

Yarborough v. Alvarado, 95–96